Essential
COSTA RICA
TRAVEL GUIDE 2025 EDITION

Complete Tips, Top Attractions, and Unique Experiences

Eric Cattaneo

Copyright © 2024 by Scott Johnson

All rights reserved. No part of this publication may be reproduced, distributed, or transmitted in any form or by any means, including photocopying, recording, or other electronic or mechanical methods, without the prior written permission of the publisher, except in the case of brief quotations embodied in critical reviews and certain other noncommercial uses permitted by copyright law.

DISCLAIMER

The information provided in this book is for general informational purposes only. All information in the book is provided in good faith, however, Scott Johnson makes no representation or warranty of any kind, express or implied, regarding the accuracy, adequacy, validity, reliability, availability, or completeness of any information in the book. Under no circumstance shall Scott Johnson have any liability to you for any loss or damage of any kind incurred as a result of the use of the book or reliance on any information provided in the book. Your use of the book and your reliance on any information in the book is solely at your own risk.

Table of contents

Chapter One: INTRODUCTION   7
  Welcome to Costa Rica   7
  Planning Your Trip   11
  Why Costa Rica is a Must-Visit Destination   15
  Best Time to Visit and What to Expect   21

Chapter Two: GETTING THERE   25
  Affordable Ways to Get to Costa Rica   25
  Flying into San José or Liberia International Airports   29
  Entry from Abroad: Visa and Travel Requirements   33
  Health and Vaccination Requirements   36
  Pros, Cons, and Parking Tips for Rental Cars   38

Chapter Three: ACCOMMODATION   43
  Throughout Costa Rica   43
  In San José   48
  In Monteverde   56
  In Manuel Antonio   59
  In Tamarindo   64
  In Puerto Viejo   68

Chapter Four: RESTAURANTS   73
  Recommended Restaurants within   73
    San José   73
    Monteverde   80
    Manuel Antonio   84
  Tamarindo   89
    Puerto Viejo   93

Chapter Five: TOP ATTRACTIONS — 106

- Beaches / Open / Close Hours (e.g., Manuel Antonio, Tamarindo) — 106
- National Parks and Wildlife Reserves (e.g., Tortuguero, Corcovado) — 111
- Waterfalls and Adventure Parks — 120
- Popular Hikes & Walks (e.g., Monteverde Cloud Forest, Tenorio National Park) — 125
- Weather and Climate — 130
- Family-Friendly Activities / Open / Close Hours — 135
- Nearby Towns and Beaches — 140

Chapter Six: EXPLORING COSTA RICA — 145

- Renting Cars and Parking — 145
- Domestic Flights and Shuttle Services — 150
- Taxi and Ride-Sharing Options — 159

Chapter Seven: PRACTICAL INFORMATION — 165

- Tourist Information Offices (Locations, Hours, Services) — 165
- Essential Maps: Navigating the Country and Major Attractions — 171
- Currency, Language, Safety, and Local Customs — 174

Chapter Eight: NEIGHBOURING TOWNS & REGIONS — 179

- San José — 179
- Liberia — 182
- Monteverde — 186
- La Fortuna — 189
- Manuel Antonio — 193
- Tamarindo — 196

Puerto Viejo	200
Nosara	204
Dominical	207
Chapter Nine: EXPERIENCE	**210**
Staying Safe in Costa Rica	210
Wildlife Watching (e.g., Sloths, Monkeys, Turtles)	214
Canopy Tours and Ziplining	219
Rafting And Kayaking Adventures	224
Surfing and Water Sports	228
Hot Springs and Spa Retreats	233
Local Cooking Classes and Food Tours	237
Chapter Ten: SHOPPING	242
Best Markets and Shops for Local Goods	242
Local Crafts, Coffee, and Unique Finds (e.g., Handmade Jewelry, Costa Rican Coffee)	247
Chapter Eleven: ITINERARIES AND TRAVEL TIPS	**252**
1 Day, 3 Day, 5 Day Suggested Itineraries	252
Essentials for Every Season (Packing and Activities)	258
Chapter Twelve: FINAL THOUGHTS	**264**
Conclusion regarding Costa Rica's Natural and Cultural Wonders	271

Chapter One:
INTRODUCTION

Welcome to Costa Rica

You have arrived in Costa Rica! As you set off on your tour, you should be ready to be enthralled by a place where the splendour of nature and the vitality of culture coexist in perfect harmony.

Costa Rica, which is sometimes referred to as the "Switzerland of Central America," is a little nation with a huge heart. It provides every kind of tourist with a wide variety of experiences that are tailored to their own interests.

You will be met with the warmth and kindness of the Ticos, the local people who exemplify the spirit of "Pura Vida," from the minute you arrive until the moment you leave. This word, which may be translated as "pure life," is more than simply a slogan; it is a way of life that symbolises the laid-back, pleasant, and accepting attitude that is prevalent in the nation. When you are in San José, whether you are visiting a distant village or traversing the busy streets of San José, you will discover that the locals are always eager to share a smile, a tale, or a helping hand with you.

Naturalists will find that Costa Rica is a paradise on earth. There is a remarkable variety of landscapes in this nation, despite the fact that it is quite tiny. These landscapes range from sun-kissed beaches and towering volcanoes to foggy cloud forests and expansive jungles.

Each location has its own particular charm and opportunity for adventure. Imagine waking up to the sound of howler monkeys in the forest, strolling through leafy paths to uncover secret waterfalls, or snorkelling in crystal-clear seas filled with marine life.

 One of the most astonishing qualities of Costa Rica is its biodiversity. The nation is home to 5% of the world's species, making it one of the most biologically intensive regions on Earth. As you explore, you'll discover a magnificent diversity of animals, from colourful toucans and lively monkeys to elusive jaguars and gentle sea turtles. National parks and animal reserves, such as Corcovado and Tortuguero, give a look into this rich natural heritage and are a must-visit for any nature lover.

For those seeking adventure, Costa Rica offers a playground of fascinating activities. Whether you're zip-lining through the trees, white-water rafting down roaring rivers, or surfing the Pacific waves, there's no lack of adrenaline-pumping thrills. The country's diverse topography offers the ideal background for outdoor pursuits, guaranteeing that every day delivers a new and fascinating challenge.

Beyond its natural beauty, Costa Rica is a nation rich in culture and history. The lively culture, music, and food represent a combination of indigenous, Spanish, and Afro-Caribbean influences. Take the opportunity to visit local markets, where you may try delectable foods like Gallo Pinto and Casado, or participate in the celebrations during one of the many colourful festivals held throughout the year.

Costa Rica is also a worldwide pioneer in sustainable tourism. The country's dedication to protecting its natural resources and developing eco-friendly activities is reflected in its wide network of protected areas and eco-lodges. By choosing to visit Costa Rica, you're supporting a location that cherishes and preserves its environment, ensuring that future generations may continue to enjoy its beauties.

As you dig into this book and begin your experience in Costa Rica, remember to embrace the spirit of "Pura Vida." Take the time to engage with the people, immerse yourself in the natural beauty, and relish every minute of your tour. Costa Rica is more than simply a destination—it's an experience that will leave you with memories to treasure for a lifetime.

Welcome to Costa Rica, where every corner contains a new discovery, and every encounter is a step closer to comprehending the genuine core of "Pura Vida." Let's explore this fascinating region together!

Planning Your Trip

Planning your vacation to Costa Rica is a thrilling journey full of anticipation and discovery. Here's a complete guide to help you prepare for a wonderful vacation to this tropical paradise.

When to Visit

Costa Rica's climate is separated into two primary seasons: the dry season and the rainy season. Each provides distinct experiences:

- **Dry Season (December to April):** This is the most popular period to come, particularly for beach lovers and outdoor enthusiasts. Expect sunny days, clear skies, and great weather for exploring the Pacific coast, hiking, and enjoying water sports.

- **Rainy Season (May to November):** Also known as the "green season," this time turns the terrain into a lush, vivid beauty. It's excellent for individuals who appreciate less crowds, reduced pricing, and the splendour of nature in full bloom. The waterfalls are especially magnificent at this season.

Getting There

Costa Rica is accessible via two major international airports:

- **Juan Santamaría International Airport (SJO) in San José:** Convenient for seeing the centre and southern areas, including the capital city and adjacent attractions.
- **Daniel Oduber Quirós International Airport (LIR)** in Liberia: Ideal for reaching the northern Pacific coast, including popular resorts like Tamarindo and the Nicoya Peninsula.

Entry Requirements

Before you go, verify the visa and entrance requirements for your country. Most travellers may enter Costa Rica without a visa for up to 90 days, but it's always advisable to check current requirements. Ensure your passport is valid for at least six months beyond your scheduled travel date.

Accommodation

Costa Rica provides a broad choice of housing alternatives to meet every budget and preference:

- **Luxury Resorts:** For those wanting a high-end experience, various luxury resorts provide world-class facilities and spectacular vistas.
- **Eco-Lodges:** Perfect for eco-conscious tourists, these lodges give a unique chance to remain close to nature while reducing your environmental effect.
- **Budget-Friendly Options:** Hostels, guesthouses, and budget hotels are commonly accessible, giving pleasant and economical accommodations.

Transportation

Getting about Costa Rica is quite straightforward, with various methods available:

- **Rental Cars:** Renting a vehicle provides you the flexibility to explore at your own speed. Be mindful of road conditions and parking suggestions, particularly in rural regions.
- **Domestic Flights:** For speedier travel across areas, consider choosing a domestic flight. Several airlines provide frequent flights to significant locations.
- **Public buses:** A cheap method to travel, public buses link most towns and cities. It's a terrific alternative if you're on a budget.
- **Shuttle Services:** Convenient and comfortable, shuttle services are provided for popular routes and may be scheduled in advance.

Packing Tips

What you carry may make a major impact in your trip experience. Here are several essentials:

- **Clothes:** Lightweight, breathable clothes for the warm temperature, and a light jacket or sweater for chilly nights. Don't forget swimsuits and good walking shoes.

- **Rain Gear:** If you're coming during the rainy season, take a waterproof jacket and an umbrella.
- **Sun Protection:** Sunscreen, sunglasses, and a hat are must-haves to protect oneself from the fierce tropical sun.
- **Insect Repellent:** Essential for keeping mosquitoes and other pests at bay, particularly in forest and coastal settings.

Planning your vacation to Costa Rica is the first step towards an amazing journey. With its spectacular natural beauty, rich culture, and infinite activities, Costa Rica offers a voyage filled with exploration and delight. Take your time to prepare, embrace the spirit of "Pura Vida," and be ready to make memories that will last a lifetime.

Why Costa Rica is a Must-Visit Destination

As I sit here remembering about my adventures across Costa Rica, I can't help but feel a surge of exhilaration flood over me. This nation, with its bright scenery and warm-hearted people, has a way of grabbing your spirit and leaving an unforgettable stamp on your heart. Let me take you on a trip through the reasons why Costa Rica is a must-visit place, sharing my own experiences and observations along the way.

A Symphony of Nature

Imagine waking up to the sound of howler monkeys in the distance, the calm rustle of foliage, and the exquisite music of tropical birds. That's how my mornings started in Costa Rica. The country's natural beauty is like a symphony, with each element playing its role to produce a harmonic experience. From the misty cloud forests of Monteverde to the sun-drenched beaches of the Nicoya Peninsula, every area of Costa Rica provides a distinct and magnificent vista.

One of my fondest memories is going through the deep forests of Corcovado National Park. The sheer range of species was stunning. I recall noticing a family of capuchin monkeys swinging through the trees, their eager gaze studying me as I walked by. The pleasure of witnessing a scarlet macaw in flight, its vivid feathers contrasted against the green canopy, is something I'll never forget.

Adventures Around Every Corner

Costa Rica is a paradise for explorers. Whether you're an adrenaline junkie or someone who loves a leisurely journey, there's something here for everyone. One of the highlights of my vacation was zip-lining among the trees in Arenal.

The adrenaline of flying over the trees, with the Arenal Volcano towering in the backdrop, was exciting. Each zip-line gave a fresh view, and the guides were wonderful, sharing their expertise about the plants and wildlife below.

For those who like water-based sports, Costa Rica's rivers and coasts are a dream. I got the opportunity to go white-water rafting on the Pacuare River, manoeuvring over exhilarating rapids while surrounded by magnificent jungle. The feeling of success and the camaraderie with other rafters made it an amazing experience.

Embracing the Pura Vida Lifestyle

"Pura Vida" is more than just a word in Costa Rica; it's a way of life. It symbolises the country's laid-back, pleasant, and friendly attitude.

During my visit, I found myself slowing down, savouring the little pleasures, and actually living in the present. The natives, or Ticos, are among the kindest people I've ever encountered. Their genuine welcome and warmth made me feel completely at home.

One evening, I was invited to a local family's house for supper. We exchanged tales, laughs, and a beautiful lunch of Gallo Pinto and fresh fish. It was a simple but powerful event that underlined the core of Pura Vida—finding pleasure in the simplest things and connecting with people.

A Commitment to Sustainability

Costa Rica's devotion to sustainability is very impressive. The government has made tremendous efforts to safeguard its natural resources and encourage eco-friendly activities. I stayed at numerous eco-lodges on my journey, each providing a distinct mix of comfort and environmental awareness. These lodges not only offered a nice place to relax but also taught visitors about conservation initiatives and sustainable living.

One such retreat was hidden on the Osa Peninsula, surrounded by lush jungle. The proprietors were dedicated to conserving the environment and included visitors in activities like tree planting and beach clean-ups. It was wonderful to see how tourism could survive with nature, helping both the local population and the ecosystem.

Cultural Richness and Diversity

Costa Rica's culture is a rich tapestry woven from indigenous, Spanish, and Afro-Caribbean elements. This rich cultural legacy is represented in the country's music, dancing, festivals, and food. I had the pleasure of visiting a local festival in the town of Liberia, where the streets came alive with colourful parades, traditional music, and dance displays. The excitement and passion of the participants were irresistible, and I found myself dancing along with the audience.

The food scene in Costa Rica is equally diversified and delicious. From street food booths dishing up delectable empanadas to upmarket restaurants providing sophisticated spins on classic meals, there's plenty to suit every appetite. One of my best culinary experiences was a cooking lesson in a tiny community, where I learnt to prepare traditional Costa Rican meals using fresh, local ingredients.

Costa Rica is a place that provides a great combination of natural beauty, adventure, cultural depth, and genuine friendliness. It's a location where you can reconnect with nature, push yourself with adventurous activities, and immerse yourself in a lively culture.

As you plan your vacation, remember to embrace the spirit of Pura Vida, take your time to explore, and cherish every minute. Costa Rica is not simply a destination; it's an experience that will leave you with memories to treasure for a lifetime.

Best Time to Visit and What to Expect

As I reflect on my trips across Costa Rica, one of the most commonly asked questions I hear is, "When is the best time to visit?" The answer, of course, depends on what type of experience you're searching for. Costa Rica is a nation of different temperatures and scenery, each providing something distinct throughout the year. Let me offer my ideas and personal experiences to help you determine the optimum time for your vacation.

The Dry Season: Sun-Kissed Adventures

The dry season, which spans from December to April, is widely considered the greatest time to visit Costa Rica, particularly if you're a sun-seeker. During these months, the weather is often warm and bright, making it excellent for beach trips and outdoor activities. I recall my first visit to the Pacific coast during the dry season. The beaches of Manuel Antonio were nothing short of paradise—golden sands, crystal blue seas, with the sun blazing brilliantly above. It was the perfect site for swimming, sunbathing, and snorkelling.

One of the pleasures of coming during the dry season is the availability of festivals and cultural activities. I got the pleasure to attend the vivid Fiestas de Palmares, a two-week-long event full of music, dancing, bullfights, and parades.

The excitement and passion of the natives were contagious, and it was a terrific opportunity to immerse oneself in Costa Rican culture.

The Green Season: Nature's Bounty

From May to November, Costa Rica enters its rainy season, often known as the green season. While some would shy away from the prospect of rain, this era has its own special appeal. The terrain changes into a lush, green utopia, and the plants and wildlife are at their most brilliant. I remember a trek in the Monteverde Cloud Forest during the green season. The forest was alive with the sounds of nature, and the foggy environment provided a beautiful touch to the encounter.

The green season is also the finest period for wildlife aficionados. The additional rainfall means rivers and waterfalls are at their fullest, and the woodlands are bursting with life. I got the great chance to see the nesting of sea turtles on the Caribbean shore. Watching these amazing animals lay their eggs under the cover of darkness was a humbling and wonderful experience.

Shoulder Seasons: The Best of Both Worlds

If you're trying to escape the peak tourist throngs and yet enjoy pleasant weather, consider going during the shoulder seasons—late November to early December and May to early June. These transitional seasons provide a combination of bright days and occasional rains, offering a balanced experience.

During my journey in early December, I had the best of both worlds: the lush foliage from the recent rains and the bright, sunny days characteristic of the dry season.

What to Expect

No matter when you visit Costa Rica, there are a few things you can always expect: friendly folks, breathtaking surroundings, and a multitude of activities to pick from. The country's numerous microclimates mean you may encounter different weather conditions within a short distance. For instance, you may start your day with a bright beach stroll in Tamarindo and conclude it with a cold, foggy evening in the Monteverde Cloud Forest.

It's also crucial to be prepared for the unexpected. Costa Rica's weather may be variable, particularly in the green season. Pack a light rain jacket and waterproof clothing, even if you're coming during the dry season. Embrace the unpredictability and allow the weather to lend an element of adventure to your journey.

Choosing the ideal time to visit Costa Rica ultimately relies on your choices and what you wish to experience. Whether you're attracted to the sun-drenched beaches of the dry season, the lush landscapes of the green season, or the balanced appeal of the shoulder seasons, Costa Rica offers an amazing adventure. Embrace the attitude of "Pura Vida," and be ready to discover a nation that provides beauty and adventure year-round.

Chapter Two: GETTING THERE

Affordable Ways to Get to Costa Rica

Planning a vacation to Costa Rica on a budget? You're in for a treat! Let me offer some of my own suggestions and experiences on how to go to this wonderful nation without breaking the wallet. From finding inexpensive tickets to exploring alternate travel choices, there are many ways to make your visit to Costa Rica both economical and fun.

Finding Cheap Flights

One of the greatest ways to save money on your vacation to Costa Rica is by landing a fantastic bargain on flights. I recall spending hours scanning the internet for the cheapest deals, and it paid off! Here are some ways that worked for me:

1. **Use Flight Comparison Websites:** Websites like Skyscanner and Kayak are wonderful for comparing airfares across numerous airlines. They let you set up price alerts, so you may be alerted when rates decrease.
2. **Be Flexible with Dates:** If your trip dates are flexible, you may typically locate cheaper

airfares. I discovered that travelling mid-week, particularly on Tuesdays and Wednesdays, tended to be less costly than weekends.

3. **Consider neighbouring Airports:** Sometimes travelling into a neighbouring airport will save you money. For example, if you're headed to the Pacific coast, check flights to both San José (SJO) and Liberia (LIR) airports. I previously saved a large sum by flying into Liberia and taking a bus to my destination.

Budget Airlines and Stopovers

While direct flights are handy, they may be pricey. I realised that selecting for flights with stopovers may drastically lower prices. On one of my excursions, I travelled with a cheap airline that had a stopover in Mexico City. Not only did I save money, but I also got to visit a new city for a few hours!

1. **Bargain Airlines:** Keep an eye out for bargain airlines that travel to Costa Rica. They generally offer cheaper rates, particularly if you're prepared to forsake some of the comforts.

2. **Stopover Bargains:** Some airlines provide stopover bargains where you may stay a day or two in the layover city at no additional expense. It's like having a mini-vacation inside your journey!

Alternative Travel Options

If you're eager for an adventure and have some additional time, investigate alternate travel choices to reach Costa Rica. These may be both cost-effective and thrilling.

1. **Overland Travel:** If you're already in Central America, travelling overland might be a terrific way to save money. Buses are a popular and economical choice. I once boarded a bus from Nicaragua to Costa Rica, and it was a fantastic adventure packed with magnificent landscapes and intriguing interactions with other passengers.
2. **Boat Travel:** For individuals visiting from adjacent countries, there are boat services that link to Costa Rica. It's a unique way to travel and gives great views of the coastline.

Travel During Off-Peak Seasons

Travelling during off-peak seasons may lead to big savings. I discovered that visiting Costa Rica during the shoulder seasons (late November to early December and May to early June) not only saved me money on airfares but also on lodgings and activities.

1. **Reduced Prices:** During certain periods, planes and hotels generally offer reduced prices to entice passengers. Plus, you'll experience fewer people and a more casual environment.
2. **Special bargains:** Keep an eye out for special bargains and promotions during certain dates. Many airlines and hotels provide discounts to promote reservations during the off-peak season.

Getting to Costa Rica on a budget is perfectly achievable with a little preparation and flexibility. By utilising airfare comparison tools, considering budget airlines and stopovers, investigating alternative travel choices, and visiting during off-peak seasons, you may make your ideal vacation to Costa Rica a reality without breaking the bank.

Flying into San José or Liberia International Airports

When planning your vacation to Costa Rica, one of the first considerations you'll need to make is which airport to fly into: San José's Juan Santamaría International Airport (SJO) or Liberia's Daniel Oduber Quirós International Airport (LIR). Both airports offer their individual benefits, and picking the proper one may set the tone for your vacation. Let me offer my own experiences and views to assist you decide.

San José - Juan Santamaría International Airport (SJO)

Flying into San José is like walking into the heart of Costa Rica. Located just outside the busy capital city, SJO is the country's biggest and busiest airport. My first arrival here was a frenzy of excitement and expectation. The airport itself is contemporary and well-equipped, with lots of facilities to make your arrival easy and pleasant.

- **Proximity to Key Destinations:** One of the main benefits of flying into San José is its central position. From here, you may quickly visit a range of places. On my first trip, I hired a vehicle and drove to the Central Pacific coast in only a couple of hours. The trip was picturesque, with rich green scenery and views of the ocean along the way. If you're headed to famous places like Manuel Antonio, Arenal Volcano, or the Caribbean coast, San José is a handy starting point.

- **Cultural Immersion:** San José itself is worth investigating. I spent a couple of days roaming around its bustling streets, seeing museums, and tasting the local food. The National Theater and the Pre-Columbian Gold Museum were highlights. Plus, the city's marketplaces are a terrific spot to pick up gifts and try classic delicacies like Gallo Pinto.

- **Transportation Options:** Getting from the airport to your destination is uncomplicated. There are many rental vehicle businesses, shuttle services, and taxis available. I found the hotel shuttle service quite useful, especially after a lengthy trip.

Liberia - Daniel Oduber Quirós International Airport (LIR)

Liberia's airport, situated in the Guanacaste area, has a different feel entirely. My initial impression of LIR was its laid-back ambiance and the pleasant, tropical wind that welcomed me as I walked off the plane. This airport is smaller and less chaotic than San José, which might provide for a more calm arriving experience.

- **Gateway to the Pacific Coast:** If your plan includes the gorgeous beaches of the Pacific coast, Liberia is the appropriate entrance point. I recall my enthusiasm as I travelled from the airport to Tamarindo, a beautiful beach town noted for its surf and sunsets. The travel was fast and lovely, and I was on the beach within an hour of landing.

- **Proximity to Natural Wonders:** Liberia is also near some of Costa Rica's most magnificent natural attractions. On one excursion, I visited the Rincon de la Vieja National Park, noted for its volcanic activity and hot springs. The park was only a short drive from the airport, and the experience of trekking through its rocky landscape and bathing in natural hot springs was amazing.

- **Less Crowded and More calm:** One of the things I appreciate about travelling into Liberia is the calm pace. The airport is less busy, and the procedure of going through customs and baggage claim is typically faster. This means you may start your holiday sooner and with less worry.

Making the Choice

Choosing between San José and Liberia relies on your trip goals and tastes. If you're hoping to visit a variety of locations and experience a combination of city life and natural beauty, San José is a terrific option. Its central position makes it simple to visit many of Costa Rica's main locations.

On the other side, if your concentration is on the Pacific coast and you want a more laid-back arrival, Liberia is excellent. It's great for beach lovers and those wishing to delve immediately into the natural treasures of Guanacaste.

Both San José and Liberia airports offer distinct benefits, and any pick will put you up for an excellent Costa Rican journey. Reflect on your plan, evaluate the activities you want to emphasise, and select the airport that most corresponds with your vacation objectives. Whether you arrive in the busy centre of San José or the calm entrance of Liberia, Costa Rica's beauty and charm greet you.

Entry from Abroad: Visa and Travel Requirements

Planning a vacation to Costa Rica is always an exciting experience, but negotiating the visa and travel formalities may often seem a little stressful. Let me offer my own experiences and advice to make this procedure as simple and clear as possible.

Visa Requirements

One of the first things I did while arranging my trip was to verify the visa requirements. Luckily, Costa Rica has a relatively basic policy for most people.

If you're from the United States, Canada, the European Union, or many other countries, you won't require a visa for visits up to 90 days. This was a tremendous relief for me, since it meant less paperwork and more time to concentrate on organising my excursions.

However, it's always a good idea to double-check the exact regulations for your nationality. I recall a buddy from South Africa who needed to apply for a visa in advance. The method was quite straightforward, although it did need some additional time and preparation. Make sure your passport is valid for at least six months beyond your scheduled departure date, since this is a typical requirement.

Proof of Economic Means

When I arrived in Costa Rica, one of the things the immigration officer asked for was confirmation of economic means. Essentially, they want to guarantee that you have enough money to maintain yourself throughout your stay. I had heard about this prior, so I was prepared with a bank statement indicating adequate cash. Generally, they want at least $100 every month of your stay, which isn't too tough to fulfil.

Return or Onward Ticket

Another key need is possessing a return or onward ticket. This is something I nearly ignored on my first trip. Costa Rican immigration authorities want to know that you have intentions to depart the country before your visa or entry stamp expires. I had a return trip scheduled, but if you're going to fly forward to another nation, make sure you have that ticket ready to display.

I once encountered a tourist who didn't have an onward ticket and had to hurriedly buy a refundable ticket at the airport to meet this requirement. It's an excellent reminder to always have your trip arrangements well-documented.

Health and Vaccination Requirements

While Costa Rica doesn't have any necessary vaccines for most tourists, it's always advisable to read the current health warnings. For instance, if you're travelling from a place with a danger of yellow fever, you'll need to provide evidence of immunisation. I didn't require any particular vaccines for my trip, but I made sure my usual immunizations were up to date.

Customs and Declarations

When you arrive in Costa Rica, you'll need to go through customs. This section was relatively basic for me. Just be honest about what you're bringing into the nation. There are tight limitations concerning some products, such fresh fruit and big sums of cash. I stated all I needed to, and the procedure was straightforward.

One item to notice is that Costa Rica has a departure tax of $29, which is generally included in your flight ticket. On one of my journeys, it wasn't included, and I had to pay for it at the airport. It's a little detail, but worth checking to prevent any last-minute shocks.

Navigating the visa and travel procedures for Costa Rica could seem a little difficult at first, but with a little planning, it's very simple. Make sure you have all your paperwork in order, check the particular criteria for your country, and be prepared to present evidence of finances and a return or onward ticket.

Costa Rica is a friendly and beautiful nation, and after you get through the admission procedure, you'll be ready to enjoy all the great adventures it has to offer. From its magnificent beaches and lush rainforests to its lively culture and friendly people, Costa Rica is a place that really offers something for everyone.

So, grab your paperwork, pack your luggage, and get ready for a wonderful trip in Costa Rica. The adventure starts the minute you step off the aircraft, and with these recommendations, you'll be well-prepared to start your vacation on the right foot. Pura Vida!

Pros, Cons, and Parking Tips for Rental Cars

Renting a vehicle in Costa Rica might be a game-changer for your trip experience. It allows the opportunity to explore at your own leisure and find hidden treasures off the usual road. However, it also comes with its own set of obstacles. Let me share my own experiences and ideas to help you determine whether renting a vehicle is the appropriate decision for your Costa Rican journey.

The Pros of Renting a Car

- **Freedom and Flexibility:**

One of the main benefits of owning a rental automobile is the freedom it affords. I recall the pleasure of starting out on an unplanned road trip to the Nicoya Peninsula. With no predetermined itinerary, I could stop anytime anything struck my eye—whether it was a hidden beach, a roadside fruit shop, or a spectacular perspective. This freedom enabled me to completely immerse myself in the splendour of Costa Rica.

- **Access to Remote Areas:**

Some of Costa Rica's most magnificent sites are off the main path. Having a vehicle made it feasible for me to explore locations like the isolated beaches of Santa Teresa and the beautiful jungles of the Osa Peninsula. Public transit choices to these locations are limited, so a rental vehicle was required for finding these hidden wonders.

- **Comfort and Convenience:**

Travelling with a rental vehicle means you can transport your bags and gear without worry. On one vacation, I packed my vehicle with surfboards, snorkelling equipment, and hiking gear, ready for whatever adventure that came my way. The simplicity of having everything I needed in the trunk made my trips much more pleasurable.

The Cons of Renting a Car

- **Navigating Road Conditions:**

Costa Rica's roadways may be hard, particularly in rural regions. I experienced everything from potholes to dirt roads to high mountain slopes. While these circumstances gave a feeling of adventure, they also needed cautious driving and a trustworthy vehicle. It's vital to find a rental automobile with high clearance and, if feasible, four-wheel drive.

- **Cost Considerations:**

Renting a vehicle may be costly, particularly when you consider insurance, gasoline, and extra costs. On one occasion, I was astonished by the necessary insurance expenses that greatly raised the whole amount. It's vital to budget for these charges and read the tiny print before renting your property.

- **Traffic and Parking:**

Driving in Costa Rica's cities, notably San José, may be unpleasant owing to high traffic and limited parking. I distinctly recall wandering the streets of San José, seeking a parking place near my hotel. It took longer than intended, and I ended up paying for a safe parking spot. In busy tourist sites, getting parking may sometimes be an issue, so it's smart to prepare ahead.

Parking Tips for Rental Cars

- **Choose Secure Parking:**

Whenever feasible, opt for secure parking lots or garages, particularly in metropolitan areas. I discovered this the hard way after parking on a street overnight and seeing a little damage on the vehicle the following morning. Secure parking gives peace of mind and eliminates the danger of damage or theft.

- **Use Hotel Parking:**

Many hotels and lodges provide free or inexpensive parking for visitors. During my time in Manuel Antonio, the hotel offered a handy parking place, which made it simple to come and go as I liked. Always check with your hotel regarding parking alternatives before you arrive.

- **Be Mindful of municipal restrictions:**

Pay attention to parking signs and municipal restrictions to prevent penalties or towing. In some municipalities, parking is banned during specific hours or days. I once parked in a location that was intended for market sellers on weekends and had to relocate my vehicle early in the morning to avoid a fine.

- **Park in Well-Lit places:**

If you need to park on the street, pick well-lit places with lots of foot activity. This decreases the danger of break-ins and makes it simpler to spot your vehicle after dark. I always felt more safe parking my vehicle in busy, well-lit places, particularly while touring unfamiliar cities.

Renting a vehicle in Costa Rica may improve your trip experience by allowing the flexibility to explore at your own speed and visit isolated areas. However, it's crucial to assess the positives and downsides and be prepared for the problems that come with driving in a foreign nation. By following these guidelines and preparing beforehand, you can make the most of your rental vehicle and have a smooth, pleasant ride around Costa Rica.

Chapter Three:
ACCOMMODATION

Throughout Costa Rica

Finding the ideal spot to stay in Costa Rica may be as thrilling as the experiences you'll go on. From magnificent resorts to small hostels, the nation provides a broad choice of hotels to meet any traveller's requirements and budget.

Let me take you on a tour through some of the greatest locations to stay, based on my own experiences and findings.

San José - The Urban Experience

San José, the busy capital, is generally the first destination for many vacationers. I recall my first night in the city, staying at a wonderful boutique hotel in the middle of downtown. The hotel had a fantastic combination of contemporary facilities and classic Costa Rican charm. The personnel were wonderfully kind, and the breakfast buffet was a lovely introduction to local food.

<u>Where to Stay</u>: If you're searching for convenience and comfort, try staying at the **Grano de Oro Hotel**. This ancient hotel provides a sumptuous experience with its nicely designed rooms and a rooftop garden. For budget tourists, **Selina San José** is a terrific alternative, giving a bustling environment and lots of opportunity to meet other travellers.

Arenal and La Fortuna - Adventure Awaits

La Fortuna, near the Arenal Volcano, is a hub for adventure enthusiasts. On my vacation, I slept at a resort with beautiful views of the volcano. Waking up to the sight of Arenal covered in morning mist was an incredible experience.

The location is great for individuals who appreciate outdoor activities like hiking, zip-lining, and hot springs.

Where to Stay: For a touch of luxury, **Tabacón Thermal Resort & Spa** is a terrific option. The resort boasts natural hot springs and lovely grounds. If you're on a budget, **Arenal Backpackers Resort** provides reasonable rooms with a vibrant environment and a fantastic pool area.

Monteverde - Cloud Forest Magic

Monteverde's cloud forests are a must-visit for nature enthusiasts. I slept in a modest eco-lodge secluded in the forest, where the sounds of nature lulled me to sleep each night. The region is famed for its biodiversity, and staying in Monteverde enables you to completely immerse yourself in the natural splendour of Costa Rica.

Where to Stay: *El Establo Mountain Hotel* provides spectacular views and nice rooms. For a more budget-friendly choice, *Monteverde Inn* has pleasant accommodations and convenient access to hiking trails.

Manuel Antonio - Beach Bliss

Manuel Antonio is noted for its stunning beaches and national park. I spent a few days here, sleeping at a seaside hotel where I could hear the waves smashing from my bed. The mix of lush vegetation and clean beaches makes this location a heaven for leisure and animal watching.

Where to Stay: *Arenas del Mar Beachfront & Rainforest Resort* provides exquisite rooms with direct beach access. For those on a tighter budget, **Hotel Verde Mar** gives inexpensive accommodations only feet from the beach.

Tamarindo - Surf and Sunsets

Tamarindo is a bustling coastal town noted for its surf culture and breathtaking sunsets. I slept at a seaside hostel that was excellent for meeting other tourists and enjoying the laid-back attitude of the town. The sunsets in Tamarindo are some of the most magnificent I've ever seen, colouring the sky in tones of orange and pink.

Where to Stay: *Cala Luna Boutique Hotel & Villas* provides a wonderful stay with gorgeous villas and a tranquil setting. For budget tourists, **Blue Trailz Hostel & Surf Camp** is a terrific location to stay, providing surf training and a welcoming community.

Puerto Viejo - Caribbean Charm

Puerto Viejo, on the Caribbean coast, has a particular appeal with its Afro-Caribbean culture and laid back attitude. I stayed in a lovely guest house surrounded by tropical vegetation. The town is great for visitors wishing to experience a different side of Costa Rica, with its reggae music, wonderful food, and lovely beaches.

Where to Stay: *Le Cameleon Boutique Hotel* provides beautiful rooms with a dash of Caribbean flare. For a more budget-friendly choice, **Rocking J's** is a popular hostel with a vibrant and varied feel.

Costa Rica's diversified landscapes and lively culture are mirrored in its vast choice of hotels. Whether you're searching for luxury, adventure, or a budget-friendly stay, there's something for everyone. Each location provides its own distinct experiences, and selecting the appropriate spot to stay may enrich your tour around this lovely nation.

In San José

San José, the bustling capital of Costa Rica, is generally the first destination for many vacationers. It's a city that provides a blend of urban energy and cultural depth, and selecting the ideal location to stay may make your vacation even more memorable. Let me offer some of my favourite lodgings in San José, along with locations, to help you plan your vacation.

Grano de Oro Hotel

Address: Calle 30, Avenida 2 y 4, San José, Costa Rica

My stay at the Grano de Oro Hotel was nothing short of wonderful. This historic hotel, housed in a renovated Victorian home, blends old-world elegance with contemporary conveniences. The rooms are attractively designed, integrating antique elements with modern facilities. I really appreciated the rooftop garden, a calm area to rest after a day of visiting the city. The on-site restaurant is popular among residents and tourists alike, delivering wonderful Costa Rican food with a gourmet flair.

Hotel Presidente

Address: Avenida Central, Calle 7, San José, Costa Rica

Located directly in the middle of downtown San José, Hotel Presidente is great for people who want to be in the thick of the activity. I stayed here on one of my travels and loved its accessibility to important sights like the National Theater and the Pre-Columbian Gold Museum. The rooms are big and contemporary, with vivid design that reflects the energetic character of the city. The rooftop bar provides beautiful views of San José, making it a fantastic location to unwind with a glass in hand.

Finca Rosa Blanca Coffee Plantation & Inn

Address: Santa Bárbara de Heredia, San José, Costa Rica

For a unique and serene vacation, I definitely suggest Finca Rosa Blanca. Although it's a little beyond the city centre, this eco-friendly inn is worth the short journey. Nestled in the mountains above San José, it provides stunning vistas and a calm respite from the rush and bustle. The inn is bordered by a coffee plantation, and I had an interesting tour that finished with a sampling of their organic coffee. The rooms are attractively furnished, each with its own creative flare, and the on-site restaurant provides farm-to-table food that promotes local products.

Park Inn by Radisson San José
Address: Ave 6, Calle 28, San José, Costa Rica

The Park Inn by Radisson is an excellent alternative for business travellers and vacationers alike. I stayed here for a business trip and found it to be really handy. The hotel has contemporary facilities, including a fitness centre and a pool, which were excellent for resting after a hectic day. The accommodations are modern and comfy, and the included breakfast buffet was a terrific way to start the day. Its central position makes it simple to explore the city, with several attractions within walking distance.

Selina San José

Address: Avenida 9, Calle 13, San José, Costa Rica

For a more budget-friendly alternative with a bustling environment, Selina San José is a terrific choice. This hostel provides a variety of accommodations, from dormitories to private rooms, appealing to varied budgets and interests. I enjoyed the common rooms, which are ideal for meeting other tourists. The hostel also provides many activities and trips, making it simple to discover San José and beyond. The on-site restaurant and bar are bustling areas to have a meal or a drink, and the whole ambiance is young and enthusiastic.

San José provides a broad choice of lodgings to accommodate any traveller's requirements and interests. Whether you're seeking luxury, convenience, or a budget-friendly stay, there's something for everyone in this bustling city. Each of these establishments has its own particular appeal and gives a comfortable base for experiencing the rich culture and exciting life of Costa Rica's capital.

In Arenal/La Fortuna

Arenal and La Fortuna are among Costa Rica's most intriguing attractions, providing a great combination of adventure, relaxation, and natural beauty. Finding the proper location to stay may improve your experience, making your vacation even more memorable. Let me offer some of my favourite lodgings in this lovely location, along with addresses, to help you organise your visit.

The Springs Resort and Spa

Address: 9 Km West of La Fortuna, Arenal, Costa Rica

Staying at The Springs Resort and Spa was like entering into a tropical paradise. This magnificent resort provides stunning views of the Arenal Volcano and a variety of facilities, including numerous hot spring pools, a full-service spa, and many on-site restaurants. I spent my days exploring the gorgeous grounds and my nights bathing in the thermal waters, which was the ideal way to relax after a day of excitement. The apartments are big and nicely designed, giving a tranquil refuge.

Arenal Observatory Lodge & Spa

Address: 22 Km West of La Fortuna, Arenal, Costa Rica

For nature enthusiasts, the Arenal Observatory Lodge & Spa is a dream come true. Nestled inside a protected natural reserve, this resort provides spectacular views of the Arenal Volcano and Lake Arenal. I slept in one of their beautiful apartments with a direct view of the volcano, and waking up to that scene was absolutely amazing. The resort boasts its own network of hiking paths, great for birding and animal observation. The on-site restaurant delivers wonderful meals created from locally sourced products, adding to the whole experience.

Tabacón Thermal Resort & Spa

Address: 13 Km West of La Fortuna, Arenal, Costa Rica

Tabacón Thermal Resort & Spa is known for its natural hot springs, which are supplied by the geothermal activity of the Arenal Volcano. My time here was nothing short of spectacular. The resort's beautifully designed gardens and cascading thermal pools provide a quiet haven. I spent hours soaking at the hot springs, surrounded by beautiful tropical greenery. The accommodations are elegant and comfy, and the service is superb. The resort also provides a choice of spa services, making it the ideal spot to indulge yourself.

Lomas del Volcán

Address: 4.5 Km West of La Fortuna, Arenal, Costa Rica

Lomas del Volcán provides a more private and rustic experience, with delightful cottages located within gorgeous gardens. Each home offers its own balcony with spectacular views of the Arenal Volcano. I appreciated the quaint, cabin-like vibe of my bungalow, which was outfitted with all the contemporary facilities I needed. The on-site restaurant delivers big meals, and the personnel are wonderfully nice and helpful. It's a terrific spot to stay if you want to be near nature while enjoying luxury and convenience.

Hotel Arenal Springs Resort & Spa

Address: 7 Km West of La Fortuna, Arenal, Costa Rica

Hotel Arenal Springs Resort & Spa provides a perfect balance of luxury and sustainability. The resort has large junior rooms with amazing views of the Arenal Volcano. I was especially pleased by their devotion to eco-friendly measures, from solar panels to organic gardens. The resort offers many hot pools, a full-service spa, and several dining choices. I got a peaceful massage at the spa and dined on great Costa Rican food at the on-site restaurant.

Arenal and La Fortuna provide a broad choice of lodgings to meet any traveller's requirements and interests. Whether you're seeking luxury, adventure, or a comfortable getaway, there's something for everyone in this gorgeous location. Each of these establishments has its own special character and offers a comfortable base for seeing the attractions of Arenal and La Fortuna.

In Monteverde

Monteverde, with its magical cloud forests and abundant biodiversity, is a paradise for nature enthusiasts and adventure seekers alike. Finding the ideal location to stay may make your vacation even more wonderful. Let me offer some of my favourite lodgings in Monteverde, along with locations, to help you plan your vacation.

Senda Monteverde Hotel

Address: 300 metres east of the Monteverde Butterfly Garden, Monteverde, Costa Rica

My stay at Senda Monteverde Hotel was an incredible experience. This eco-friendly boutique hotel is set in the heart of Monteverde, providing luxury rooms with a strong dedication to sustainability. The rooms are big and attractively constructed, with huge windows that allow in lots of natural light and give great views of the surrounding forest. The on-site restaurant provides great farm-to-table food, and the staff are extremely pleasant and helpful. It's the ideal spot to unwind and immerse yourself in nature.

Hotel Belmar

Address: 300 metres north of the Monteverde Cheese Factory, Monteverde, Costa Rica

Hotel Belmar is a jewel in Monteverde, blending rustic beauty with contemporary conveniences. I slept in one of their chalet-style rooms, which had a lovely, alpine vibe with a private balcony overlooking the verdant environment. The hotel's health centre provides yoga lessons and spa treatments, which were excellent for resting after a day of exploration. The restaurant provides organic, locally produced food, and the craft brewery on-site is a must-visit for beer fans. The hotel's location is perfect for exploring the Monteverde Cloud Forest Reserve and other surrounding attractions.

Monteverde Lodge & Gardens

Address: 200 metres east of the Monteverde Butterfly Garden, Monteverde, Costa Rica

Monteverde Lodge & grounds provides a tranquil refuge with beautifully designed grounds and comfortable lodgings. I appreciated the calm setting and the possibility to view nature straight from my accommodation. The lodge's restaurant provides wonderful meals, and the staff are informed about the surrounding region and willing to assist organise your activities. The resort also provides guided excursions of the cloud forest, which I found really educational and fulfilling.

El Establo Mountain Hotel

Address: 1 km east of the Monteverde Cheese Factory, Monteverde, Costa Rica

El Establo Mountain Hotel is one of the biggest and most elegant hotels in Monteverde. My time here was distinguished by spectacular views of the Gulf of Nicoya and the neighbouring mountains. The hotel provides a variety of facilities, including two swimming pools, a spa, and many restaurants. The apartments are big and nicely equipped, with huge windows that give spectacular views. The hotel's position makes it simple to visit the adjacent cloud forests and adventure parks.

Trapp Family Lodge

Address: 1 km west of the Monteverde Cloud Forest Reserve, Monteverde, Costa Rica

For a more private and family-friendly experience, the Trapp Family Lodge is a superb alternative. This beautiful lodge is situated adjacent to the Monteverde Cloud Forest Reserve, making it a great location for nature hikes and birding. I slept in a comfortable room with wooden furniture and a separate terrace. The lodge's restaurant delivers delicious, home-cooked meals, and the personnel are wonderfully kind and helpful. The tranquil surroundings and friendly friendliness made my time here absolutely unforgettable.

Monteverde provides a broad choice of hotels to accommodate any traveller's requirements and interests. Whether you're searching for luxury, rustic charm, or a family-friendly escape, there's something for everyone in this fascinating location. Each of these establishments has its own distinct character and offers a comfortable base for experiencing the marvels of Monteverde.

In Manuel Antonio

Manuel Antonio, with its magnificent beaches and thick jungles, is one of Costa Rica's most popular locations. Finding the appropriate location to stay may make your vacation even more memorable. Let me offer some of my favourite lodgings in Manuel Antonio, along with locations, to help you plan your vacation.

Gaia Hotel & Nature Reserve

Address: Quepos-Manuel Antonio Road, Manuel Antonio, Costa Rica

My stay at Gaia Hotel & Nature Reserve was an adventure in luxury and quiet. This eco-friendly, adults-only resort is situated in the jungle, providing spectacular vistas and a quiet environment. The rooms are large and attractively constructed, with individual balconies that overlook the verdant environment. The on-site restaurant delivers gourmet food, and the spa offers a selection of treatments that left me feeling invigorated. The hotel's dedication to sustainability and conservation is visible in every aspect, making it a wonderful option for eco-conscious tourists.

Hotel Costa Verde

Address: Km 5 Road to Manuel Antonio, Manuel Antonio, Costa Rica

Hotel Costa Verde is a unique and pleasant location to stay, particularly if you're seeking something a little unusual. The hotel is famed for its converted Boeing 727 aircraft suite, which provides a one-of-a-kind accommodation experience. I stayed in one of their regular rooms, which was roomy and comfortable, with a balcony that afforded wonderful views of the Pacific Ocean. The hotel is bordered by thick forest, and I regularly noticed monkeys and other animals directly from my balcony. The on-site eateries provide a range of delectable alternatives, and the closeness to Manuel Antonio National Park is a significant benefit.

Arenas del Mar Beachfront & Rainforest Resort

Address: Playa Playitas Manuel Antonio, Manuel Antonio, Costa Rica

Arenas del Mar Beachfront & jungle Resort combines the best of both worlds: immediate beach access and a gorgeous jungle setting. My time here was nothing short of wonderful. The resort's position on a cliffside affords stunning views of the ocean and the surrounding vegetation. The apartments are elegant and well-appointed, with private patios that are great for viewing the sunset. The resort's devotion to sustainability is outstanding, and the personnel are wonderfully nice and attentive. The on-site restaurant provides wonderful, locally produced food, while the spa offers a selection of calming treatments.

Si Como No Resort & Wildlife Refuge

Address: Manuel Antonio Road, Manuel Antonio, Costa Rica

Si Como No Resort & Wildlife Refuge is a terrific alternative for families and environment enthusiasts. The resort is nestled inside a nature sanctuary, and I liked waking up to the sounds of birds and monkeys.

The rooms are wide and pleasant, with balconies that give spectacular views of the forest and the ocean. The resort includes numerous pools, including a family pool with a waterslide and an adults-only pool for a more serene experience. The on-site restaurants provide a range of tasty food, and the personnel are wonderfully nice and helpful. The resort also provides a choice of activities and trips, making it simple to explore the local region.

La Mariposa Hotel

Address: Manuel Antonio Road, Manuel Antonio, Costa Rica

La Mariposa Hotel is recognized for its breathtaking panoramic views of the Pacific Ocean and Manuel Antonio National Park. My time here was amazing, owing to the hotel's stunning surroundings and outstanding service. The apartments are nicely designed, with huge windows that give spectacular views.

The infinity pool is a feature, giving a fantastic area to relax and take in the views. The on-site restaurant delivers wonderful meals, and the personnel are helpful and pleasant. The hotel's position makes it convenient to visit the local beaches and national park.

Manuel Antonio provides a broad choice of hotels to meet any traveller's requirements and interests. Whether you're seeking luxury, unusual experiences, or family-friendly alternatives, there's something for everyone in this lovely location. Each of these establishments has its own special character and gives a comfortable base for experiencing the marvels of Manuel Antonio.

In Tamarindo

Tamarindo, with its magnificent beaches, active nightlife, and laid-back feel, is a must-visit location in Costa Rica. Finding the appropriate location to stay may make your vacation even more memorable. Let me offer some of my favourite lodgings in Tamarindo, along with locations, to help you plan your vacation.

Cala Luna Boutique Hotel & Villas

Address: Playa Langosta, Tamarindo, Costa Rica

My stay at Cala Luna Boutique Hotel & Villas was an adventure in luxury and quiet. Nestled in a peaceful spot only a short walk from the beach, our hotel provides a great combination of comfort and nature. The suites and villas are elegantly furnished, with individual terraces that overlook verdant gardens. I appreciated the calm setting and the possibility to view nature directly from my balcony. The on-site restaurant provides great farm-to-table food, and the staff are extremely pleasant and helpful. It's the ideal location to rest and unwind.

Hotel Tamarindo Diria Beach Resort

Address: Tamarindo Beach, Tamarindo, Costa Rica

Hotel Tamarindo Diria Beach Resort is a terrific option if you want to be right in the middle of the activity. Located on Tamarindo Beach, this resort provides beautiful ocean views and convenient access to the town's busy entertainment and eating scene. I slept in an oceanfront hotel, and waking up to the sound of the waves was a highlight of my vacation. The resort offers various pools, including an adults-only pool, and many restaurants and bars. The breakfast buffet was a terrific way to start the day, with a large selection of things to choose from.

Capitán Suizo Beachfront Boutique Hotel

Address: Playa Tamarindo, Tamarindo, Costa Rica

Capitán Suizo Beachfront Boutique Hotel is a jewel for anyone wishing to immerse themselves in nature without compromising luxury. This eco-friendly hotel is positioned directly on the beach, surrounded by tropical gardens that attract a variety of species. I slept in a hut that was only feet from the beach, and the experience was nothing short of spectacular. The hotel's restaurant delivers wonderful dishes with an emphasis on local products, and the personnel are extremely nice and helpful. The beachside location and tranquil surroundings make it an ideal option for a relaxed break.

Wyndham Tamarindo

Address: Tamarindo, Guanacaste, Costa Rica

Wyndham Tamarindo provides a combination of contemporary facilities and spectacular vistas. Perched on a hill above the ocean, the hotel gives magnificent views of Tamarindo Bay. I stayed in a huge apartment with a private balcony, and the sunsets were incredibly spectacular. The hotel offers a stunning infinity pool, a full-service spa, and an on-site restaurant that serves a range of foreign foods. The daily shuttle service to the beach and town centre was a great amenity that made visiting Tamarindo simple and stress-free.

La Botella de Leche Hostel

Address: Calle Guanacaste, Tamarindo, Costa Rica

For budget visitors and backpackers, La Botella de Leche Hostel is a good alternative. This colourful hostel provides a pleasant and sociable environment, making it simple to meet other visitors. I slept in a private room that was clean and comfortable, with access to communal amenities including a kitchen and a pool. The hostel offers many events and trips, which makes it simple to explore the region and meet new acquaintances. The staff were really helpful and gave fantastic ideas for area eateries and activities.

Tamarindo provides a broad choice of lodgings to accommodate any traveller's requirements and interests. Whether you're seeking luxury, beachside pleasure, or a budget-friendly vacation, there's something for everyone in this busy seaside town. Each of these locations has its own special character and gives a comfortable base for experiencing the marvels of Tamarindo.

In Puerto Viejo

Puerto Viejo, tucked on Costa Rica's Caribbean coast, is a thriving town noted for its magnificent beaches, rich culture, and laid-back feel. Finding the appropriate spot to stay here might make your vacation even more memorable. Let me take you on a tour through some of my favourite hotels in Puerto Viejo, complete with locations, to help you plan your vacation.

Le Cameleon Boutique Hotel

Address: Playa Cocles, Puerto Viejo, Costa Rica

Le Cameleon Boutique Hotel is a beautiful refuge surrounded by lush tropical gardens. I recall my time here vividly—the contemporary, minimalist design of the rooms, each with a splash of lively colour, provided a tranquil and fashionable ambiance. The hotel is only a short walk from Playa Cocles, where I spent my days lazing on the beach and my nights enjoying the hotel's gourmet restaurant. The personnel were exceedingly attentive, making sure every element of my stay was excellent.

Umami Hotel

Address: Calle 219A, Puerto Viejo, Costa Rica

Umami Hotel is a hidden treasure in the heart of Puerto Viejo. This adults-only boutique hotel provides a serene vacation with its trendy, modern décor and verdant grounds. I slept in a huge apartment with a private patio overlooking the pool, and it was the ideal setting to rest after a day of exploration. The hotel's location is great, only a short walk from the town's busy entertainment and culinary scene. The on-site restaurant provides wonderful fusion food, and the personnel are pleasant and inviting.

Hotel Banana Azul

Address: Playa Negra, Puerto Viejo, Costa Rica

Hotel Banana Azul is a wonderful seaside hotel that provides a relaxing and welcoming ambiance. My time here was memorable, owing to the hotel's stunning position on Playa Negra and its helpful personnel. The accommodations are modest and rustic, with individual balconies that give wonderful views of the ocean.

I liked beginning my mornings with a fantastic breakfast on the beach and spent my afternoons lazing by the pool. The hotel's restaurant delivers fresh, locally produced food, and the bar is a perfect spot to have a beverage while watching the sunset.

Selina Puerto Viejo

Address: Calle 256, Puerto Viejo, Costa Rica

For a more budget-friendly alternative with a busy social scene, Selina Puerto Viejo is a terrific choice. This hostel provides a variety of accommodations, from dormitories to private rooms, appealing to varied budgets and interests.

I slept in a private room that was clean and comfortable, with access to communal amenities including a kitchen and a pool. The hostel arranges numerous events and trips, making it easier to explore the region and meet new tourists. The on-site restaurant and bar are bustling areas to have a meal or a drink, and the whole ambiance is young and enthusiastic.

Cariblue Beach & Jungle Resort

Address: Playa Cocles, Puerto Viejo, Costa Rica

Cariblue Beach & Jungle Resort provides a unique combination of beach and jungle activities. I slept in a wonderful home surrounded by lush tropical plants, only a short walk from the beach. The resort's position is great for visiting both the ocean and the neighbouring jungle.

The rooms are spacious and well-appointed, with individual patios that provide a serene getaway. The on-site restaurant provides great Caribbean-inspired food, and the personnel are nice and helpful. The resort also provides a choice of activities, from yoga sessions to guided nature hikes.

Puerto Viejo provides a broad choice of hotels to accommodate any traveller's requirements and interests. Whether you're seeking luxury, seaside pleasure, or a budget-friendly vacation, there's something for everyone in this busy town. Each of these locations has its own special character and offers a comfortable base for experiencing the marvels of Puerto Viejo.

Chapter Four:
RESTAURANTS

Recommended Restaurants within

San José

San José, the busy capital of Costa Rica, is a gastronomic treasure trove waiting to be discovered. From native Costa Rican meals to international cuisine, the city's eating scene is as broad as it is excellent. Let me take you on a tour of some of my favourite restaurants in San José, each delivering a distinct eating experience.

Restaurante Silvestre

Address: Ave. 11 Calle 3A - 955, San José, Costa Rica

Restaurante Silvestre is a gastronomic treasure that I came across during one of my excursions to San José. This fine dining restaurant, set in a beautifully restored colonial mansion, provides a cuisine that honours Costa Rican dishes with a contemporary touch. Chef Santiago Fernández curates a seasonal cuisine that spotlights the finest local ingredients. I was especially thrilled by the tasting menu, which took me on a gourmet voyage across the varied areas of Costa Rica. The environment is excellent for a romantic supper or a special event, and the service is superb.

Sapore Trattoria

Address: Avenida 2, San José, Costa Rica

For a taste of Italy in the heart of San José, Sapore Trattoria is the place to go. This quaint restaurant provides a comfortable and pleasant ambiance, with a menu that emphasises traditional Italian cuisine created from scratch. I recall loving their handmade pasta, which was cooked to perfection and coupled with a deep, savoury sauce. The wood-fired pizzas are also a must-try, with a crispy crust and fresh toppings. The courteous personnel and welcoming environment make Sapore Trattoria a fantastic setting for a leisurely supper with friends or family.

Restaurante Grano de Oro

Address: Calle 30, Avenida 2 y 4, San José, Costa Rica

Restaurante Grano de Oro, housed inside the beautiful Grano de Oro Hotel, is a dining experience not to be missed. The restaurant's French-inspired food is matched with a lovely location, with an open-air patio and abundant foliage. I spent a lovely supper here, beginning with the escargot and continuing on to the tenderloin steak, which was cooked to perfection. The dessert selection is also outstanding, with indulgent choices like the chocolate fondant. The attentive service and classy environment make it a fantastic option for a memorable night out.

Soda Tala

Address: Calle 3, San José, Costa Rica

For a more authentic Costa Rican eating experience, Soda Tala is a must-visit. This neighbourhood staple delivers substantial, home-cooked meals at moderate costs. I appreciated the informal, no-frills setting and the pleasant service. The menu contains typical Costa Rican cuisine including casado, a plate of rice, beans, plantains, salad, and your choice of meat. I chose the chicken casado, which was tasty and fulfilling. Soda Tala is the best spot to sample traditional Costa Rican food in a relaxing environment.

Tin Jo

Address: Calle 11, San José, Costa Rica

Tin Jo is an excellent alternative for people desiring Asian food. This family-run restaurant provides a broad cuisine that covers numerous Asian nations, including China, Japan, Thailand, and India. I was amazed by the variety of meals and the quality of the ingredients. My favourite was the Thai green curry, which was rich and fragrant, with just the proper amount of spiciness. The restaurant's atmosphere is sophisticated and tranquil, making it a fantastic setting for a relaxed supper. The personnel are informed and helpful, guaranteeing a wonderful eating experience.

San José's food scene is a fascinating combination of classic and modern cuisines, giving something for every pallet. Whether you're in the mood for sophisticated dining, Italian classics, or local Costa Rican specialties, the city offers it all. Each of these restaurants delivers a distinct eating experience, highlighting the best of what San José has to offer.

Arenal/La Fortuna

When I first arrived in La Fortuna, the bustling food scene instantly intrigued me. Nestled in the shadow of the spectacular Arenal Volcano, this lovely town provides a delicious selection of culinary experiences that appeal to every appetite. Here are some of my personal favourites that you really must try.

<u>Pollo Fortuneño</u>

One of my first destinations was Pollo Fortuneño, a local jewel famed for its delectable roast chicken. The perfume of well seasoned chicken floating through the air is tempting. I recall sitting down at a nice table, the pleasant staff greeting me with warm grins. The chicken was delicious, with a crispy skin that had just the proper amount of flavour. Paired with traditional sides like rice and beans, it was a dinner that felt like a reassuring embrace from a close friend.

Restaurante Mi Casa

For a taste of real Costa Rican food, Restaurante Mi Casa is a must-visit. Located only a short drive from the town centre, this lovely cafe provides a delicious combination of local and foreign food. I was especially delighted with their casado, a classic Costa Rican dinner that includes rice, beans, plantains, salad, and a choice of meat. The tastes were vivid and fresh, each mouthful a monument to the rich culinary tradition of the area.

Lava Lounge Bar & Grill

If you're in the mood for a vibrant environment, go over to Lava Lounge Bar & Grill. This location soon became one of my favourites for its easy going feel and live music on weekends. The cuisine is broad, appealing to both meat eaters and vegetarians. I couldn't resist sampling their famed drinks, each one a colourful mix that was as beautiful to look at as it was to consume. The live music gave a festive touch, making it a fantastic location to relax after a day of exploration.

Restaurante Rain Forest & Coffee House

For a more tranquil eating experience, Restaurante Rain Forest & Coffee House is the place to go. Nestled within beautiful vegetation, this restaurant provides a calm getaway from the hustle and bustle of town. I enjoyed beginning my mornings here with a cup of their creamy, fragrant coffee, along with a full breakfast. The menu contains a range of cuisines, but their fresh seafood selections stuck out to me. The grilled fish, delivered with a side of tropical fruits, was a highlight of my vacation.

Mercadito Arenal

Lastly, for those who prefer a little of diversity, Mercadito Arenal is a gourmet food court that provides something for everyone. From tacos and sushi to burgers and pizzas, this establishment has it all. I really appreciated the informal, laid-back environment, great for a pleasant supper with friends or family. The Voodoo Mixology Bar, situated inside the food court, offers up some of the most unique drinks I've ever had. The dry ice effect was a wonderful addition, making each sip an Instagram-worthy moment.

Exploring the gastronomic pleasures of La Fortuna was an excursion in itself. Each restaurant gave a distinct experience, representing the rich cultural fabric of this wonderful area. Whether you're a gourmet seeking for your next great meal or just someone who likes fine cuisine in a beautiful location, La Fortuna's dining scene is guaranteed to leave you satiated and wanting for more.

Monteverde

Monteverde, with its rich cloud forests and calm vistas, is a paradise for environment enthusiasts. But what genuinely shocked me was the bustling food scene that greeted me. From comfortable cafés to sophisticated dining, Monteverde provides a fascinating choice of eateries that appeal to every taste. Here are some of my personal favourites that made my stay memorable.

San Lucas Treetop Dining Experience

Address: Cerro Plano, Monteverde

Imagine eating high up in the trees, surrounded by the sounds of the wild. San Lucas Treetop Dining Experience delivers exactly that. The environment is stunning, with shimmering lights and a panoramic view of the lush foliage. I recall relishing their tasting menu, each meal a lovely reflection of Costa Rican tastes. The mix of native foods with modern methods was a gourmet adventure I won't soon forget. The highlight for me was the dessert, a rich chocolate masterpiece that nicely rounded off the evening.

Taco Taco Taqueria

Address: Santa Elena, Monteverde

For a more informal but equally pleasant experience, Taco Taco Taqueria is a must-visit. This colourful eatery is famed for its superb tacos, brimming with fresh ingredients and robust flavours. I appreciated the laid-back vibe, with colourful design and pleasant service. My favourite was the fish taco, crunchy and tasty, topped with a tangy slaw that provided the right crunch. Pair that with one of their cool margaritas, and you have a lunch that's both delicious and enjoyable.

The Green Restaurant

Address: Cerro Plano, Monteverde

Health-conscious guests will discover a refuge at The Green Restaurant. This eatery rapidly became one of my go-to locations for its nutritious and excellent options. The menu is filled with fresh, locally-sourced ingredients, and the meals are as gorgeous as they are good. I really loved their quinoa salad, a vivid blend of veggies, almonds, and a zesty vinaigrette that was both refreshing and nourishing. The calm atmosphere, with huge windows overlooking the vegetation, made it an ideal area to unwind and rejuvenate.

Choco Café Restaurant and Coffee Shop

Address: Santa Elena, Monteverde

No vacation to Monteverde would be complete without indulging in some local coffee and chocolate. Choco Café Restaurant and Coffee Shop is the ideal venue to do exactly that. The scent of freshly made coffee welcomes you as you walk in, and the warm ambiance urges you to remain around. I spent many mornings here, sipping on thick, scented coffee and relishing their exquisite pastries. Their chocolate cake is a must-try, a rich and delicious dessert that goes nicely with a cup of their trademark brew.

Monteverde Brewing Company

Address: Cerro Plano, Monteverde

For those who enjoy a decent craft beer, Monteverde Brewing Company is a jewel. This brewery provides a superb assortment of locally created beers, each with its own distinct taste character. I appreciated the calm feel of the venue, with its rustic design and pleasant clients. The personnel are enthusiastic about their art and willing to share their expertise. I really appreciated their IPA, a hoppy and refreshing beer that was excellent after a day of touring. Pair it with one of their hefty burgers, and you have a dinner that's both filling and tasty.

Restaurante Celajes at Hotel Belmar

Address: Hotel Belmar, Monteverde

For a fantastic dining experience, Restaurante Celajes at Hotel Belmar is unrivalled. The beautiful location, with breathtaking views of the surrounding scenery, sets the atmosphere for an outstanding supper. The menu provides a combination of foreign and Costa Rican cuisine, with a focus on fresh, local ingredients. I was especially delighted by their seafood dishes, each one perfectly cooked and brimming with flavour. The service was superb, making the overall meal experience genuinely exceptional.

Monteverde's food culture is as broad and active as its natural splendour. Each restaurant provides a distinct experience, reflecting the rich cultural fabric of this wonderful area. Whether you're a gourmet seeking for your next great meal or just someone who likes fine cuisine in a beautiful location, Monteverde's dining scene is guaranteed to leave you satiated and wanting for more.

Manuel Antonio

Manuel Antonio, with its magnificent beaches and thick jungles, is not simply a sanctuary for environment lovers but also a refuge for cuisine connoisseurs. The food scene here is as active and diversified as the fauna. During my vacation, I had the opportunity of eating at several absolutely great venues. Here are my top suggestions that you just must experience.

Victoria's Gourmet Italian Restaurant

Address: 618 – Diagonally Across From Tulemar, Manuel Antonio

One evening, needing some comfort food, I came into Victoria's Gourmet Italian Restaurant. The environment was warm and welcoming, with soft lighting and the fragrance of freshly made bread floating through the air.

I chose to sample their trademark pasta dish, and it did not disappoint. The pasta was exactly al dente, and the sauce was thick and savoury, with just the proper amount of garlic and herbs. The live music provided a nice touch, making it a memorable eating experience.

Puerto Escondido

Address: Hotel Playa Espadilla, Manuel Antonio

For a taste of local food, Puerto Escondido at Hotel Playa Espadilla is a must-visit. The restaurant is tucked inside a magnificent garden, giving a calm and scenic atmosphere. I recall having the ceviche, which was wonderfully fresh and acidic, paired with crunchy plantain chips. The seafood here is top-notch, and the courteous service made me feel right at home. It's the ideal area to relax after a day of visiting the national park.

Hola India Restaurant Manuel Antonio

Address: 100 Metros Norte de Tulemar Resort (Antigua Kapi Kapi), Manuel Antonio

Craving something new, I stepped inside Hola India Restaurant. The vivid design and the delicious smells of spices quickly took me to another dimension. I chose the butter chicken, and it was a revelation. The chicken was tender, and the sauce was creamy and filled with flavour. They also provide a number of vegan and vegetarian alternatives, making it a wonderful choice for everyone. The service was helpful and eager to tweak the spice level to my desire.

El Avión

Address: Manuel Antonio, Quepos

El Avión is not simply a restaurant; it's an experience. Housed in a converted Fairchild C-123 aircraft, this unusual diner provides breathtaking views of the Pacific Ocean. I opted to order their seafood plate, which was a feast for the senses. The shrimp, fish, and calamari were all cooked to perfection, and the tropical drinks were the ideal compliment. The sunset views from the balcony are incredibly beautiful, making it a must-visit site.

Emilio's Cafe

Address: Manuel Antonio, Quepos

For a more laid-back feel, Emilio's Cafe is the place to be. This quaint café provides a range of tasty food, from substantial breakfasts to light lunches. I really loved their avocado toast, topped with fresh tomatoes and a sprinkle of balsamic sauce. The coffee here is superb, obtained from local farmers and prepared to perfection. The casual environment and pleasant service make it a fantastic destination to start your day.

Falafel Bar

Address: Calle Principal, Manuel Antonio

If you're in the mood for something fast and flavorful, Falafel Bar is a terrific option. Located in the centre of Manuel Antonio, this small treasure dishes you some of the greatest falafel I've ever eaten. The pita bread was warm and fluffy, and the falafel was crunchy on the exterior and soft on the inside. They also provide a choice of fresh salads and handmade sauces that nicely compliment the entrees. It's a terrific setting for a casual supper or a fast snack.

Manuel Antonio's eating scene is a fascinating combination of native tastes and foreign cuisines. Each restaurant provides a distinct experience, representing the rich cultural tapestry of this lovely area. Whether you're a gourmet seeking for your next great meal or just someone who likes fine cuisine in a lovely environment, Manuel Antonio's restaurants are guaranteed to leave you satiated and wanting for more.

Tamarindo

Tamarindo, with its beautiful beaches and active nightlife, is a heaven for both surfers and cuisine lovers. During my visit, I had the opportunity of experiencing some of the greatest eating locations this busy town has to offer. Here are my top suggestions that you just must experience.

Dragonfly Bar & Grill

Address: Behind Hotel Pasatiempo, Tamarindo

One evening, I found myself at Dragonfly Bar & Grill, a delightful location nestled away from the busy main street. The environment was intimate and romantic, with shimmering fairy lights and a nice wind from the neighbouring seaside. I opted to sample their seafood risotto, and it was a revelation. The rice was properly cooked, creamy, and full with fresh fish tastes. The personnel were wonderfully nice, making me feel perfectly at home. It was the ideal location to relax after a day of beach activity.

El Coconut

Address: Main Street, Tamarindo Beach

For a taste of sophistication, El Coconut is a must-visit. The restaurant's stunning teak terracing and handcrafted wood furniture provide a warm and welcoming ambiance. I recall delighting in their tropical lobster, a dish cooked with fresh pineapple, raisins, and ginger. The blend of tastes was superb, and the presentation was equally outstanding. The customised attention from the personnel made the meal experience even more remarkable. It's a location where you can fully relax and enjoy a great dinner.

Pangas Beach Club

Address: North Tamarindo Beach, Tamarindo

Pangas Beach Club provides a unique dining experience directly on the dunes of Tamarindo Beach. I appreciated the easygoing mood throughout the day, great for getting a refreshing drink in my board shorts. By night, the venue changes into a romantic restaurant with candlelight tables and a wonderful view of the ocean. I couldn't resist their seafood plate, which contained shrimp, salmon, and calamari, all cooked to perfection. The tropical drinks were a great bonus, making it a fantastic evening by the water.

Patagonia Argentinian Grill & Restaurant

Address: Calle del Parque, Tamarindo

For a taste of Argentina in Costa Rica, Patagonia Argentinian Grill & Restaurant is the place to go. The rich aromas of their grilled meats are just tempting. I recall loving their trademark steak, which was soft and juicy, cooked to perfection with their particular marinades. The warm and friendly ambiance, complemented with superb service, made it a dining experience to remember. They also provide a selection of vegetarian and seafood alternatives, ensuring there's something for everyone.

NOI Bistro

Address: Avenida Central Plaza, Tamarindo

For breakfast aficionados, NOI Bistro is a hidden treasure. This lovely café provides a great choice of breakfast dishes that will have you coming back for more. I really loved their EL NOI BF, which includes two eggs, fresh bread, hash browns, bacon, and Pico de Gallo. The quantities were big, and the tastes were right on. The relaxing environment and polite service made it a fantastic site to start my day before venturing out to explore Tamarindo.

Green Papaya Taco Bar

Address: Calle Central, Tamarindo

If you're in the mood for some tasty tacos, Green Papaya Taco Bar is the place to go. This lively eatery serves a variety of tacos, each overflowing with fresh ingredients and robust tastes. I adored the beef burrito, which was stuffed with delicious meat and topped with a tangy salsa. The bright design and laid-back feel made it a great location to hang out with friends. Their delicious margaritas were the ideal companion to the dinner, making it a very pleasurable dining experience.

Tamarindo's food culture is as broad and intriguing as its natural beauty. Each restaurant provides a distinct experience, reflecting the rich cultural fabric of this dynamic town. Whether you're a gourmet seeking for your next great meal or just someone who likes fine cuisine in a beautiful location, Tamarindo's dining scene is guaranteed to leave you satiated and wanting for more.

Puerto Viejo

Exploring the food scene in Puerto Viejo is an excursion in itself. The town's rich blend of ethnicities is mirrored in its variety and superb cuisine options. Let me take you on a tour of some of my favourite eateries in Puerto Viejo, each with its own distinct charm and tastes.

Cafe Rico

Address: Puerto Viejo Downtown, Puerto Viejo, Costa Rica

Cafe Rico is my go-to destination for breakfast in Puerto Viejo. Tucked away in a charming nook of downtown, this rustic and bohemian café is a sanctuary for book lovers and foodies alike. The walls are lined with books, providing a warm and friendly ambiance. My favourite meal here is the "Ana Rosa Special," a substantial breakfast plate with avocado, eggs, fried yellow onions, ham pieces, sweet plantain, mushrooms, and beet. It's the best way to start the day, particularly if you have a big trip ahead. Just remember, Cafe Rico is closed on Thursdays and Fridays, so plan accordingly.

Stashus con Fusion

Address: Main Road, Between Sloth Toes and Cafe Viejo, Puerto Viejo de Talamanca, Costa Rica

Stashus en combination is a gastronomic jewel that delivers a delicious combination of Caribbean and Asian tastes. Located just south of town, this eatery is a must-visit for anybody eager to experience something unusual. The menu contains a range of vegetable meals, as well as tofu and tempeh alternatives. I definitely suggest the Indian curry and the Jamaican spicy stir-fry. The vivid tastes and inventive mixes make every meal a gastronomic delight. The calm, open-air atmosphere adds to the whole experience, making it an ideal site for a leisurely supper.

KOKi Beach Restaurant & Bar

Address: Avenida 71, Puerto Viejo, Costa Rica

KOKi Beach Restaurant & Bar is a bustling seaside place that provides a superb dining experience. The restaurant's open-air architecture and bright furnishings create a lively and casual environment. I love coming here for dinner and drinks, particularly to appreciate the amazing ocean views. The menu comprises a mix of Caribbean and foreign meals, with a focus on fresh, locally sourced ingredients. My favourite meal is the seafood paella, which is filled with flavour and expertly prepared. The beverages are also top-notch, making KOKi Beach a perfect location to relax after a day of touring.

El Refugio Grill

Address: Playa Negra, Puerto Viejo, Costa Rica

El Refugio Grill is a hidden treasure found near Playa Negra. This modest, family-run restaurant provides a comfortable and private eating experience. The menu concentrates on grilled meats and seafood, with a range of delectable alternatives to pick from. I had the pleasure of eating their steak, which was cooked to perfection and presented with a tasty chimichurri sauce. The chocolate brownie with ice cream for dessert was the ideal way to cap the meal. The courteous service and casual environment make El Refugio Grill a must-visit location in Puerto Viejo.

Bread & Chocolate

Address: Calle 215, Puerto Viejo, Costa Rica

Bread & Chocolate is a wonderful bistro that specialises in fresh baked foods and delectable sweets. It's the ideal location to indulge your sweet craving or have a leisurely breakfast. I typically stop by for their renowned chocolate cake, which is rich, moist, and incredibly excellent. The café also provides a range of savoury alternatives, including sandwiches and salads. The laid-back attitude and courteous personnel make Bread & Chocolate a fantastic area to unwind and enjoy a treat.

Puerto Viejo's food sector is as broad and active as the municipality itself. From substantial breakfasts at Cafe Rico to the fusion tastes of Stashus with Fusion, there's something for every pallet. Whether you're searching for a vibrant beachside restaurant or a nice, personal dining experience, Puerto Viejo offers it all. Each of these eateries delivers a distinct sense of the town's rich cultural past and culinary inventiveness.

Local Costa Rican Cuisine (e.g., Gallo Pinto, Casado)

Costa Rica's gastronomic scene is a colourful tapestry of tastes, firmly anchored in history and culture. During my travels, I had the pleasure of plunging into the heart of Costa Rican food, eating meals that are both comfortable and brimming with flavour. Here are some of the local favourites that you definitely must taste.

- **Gallo Pinto**

My mornings in Costa Rica generally started with the lovely scent of Gallo Pinto. This classic breakfast meal is a mainstay in every Costa Rican family. It's a simple but delectable blend of rice and black beans, sautéed with onions, sweet peppers, and cilantro. The first time I tried it, I was astonished by its hearty and gratifying quality. Often served with scrambled or fried eggs, fried plantains, and a dollop of natilla (a sort of sour cream), Gallo Pinto rapidly became my go-to breakfast. The addition of Salsa Lizano, an acidic and somewhat sweet salsa, lifted the meal to new heights. It's the ideal way to start the day, offering a surge of energy and taste.

- **Casado**

For lunch, nothing surpasses a typical Casado. The term "Casado" means "married," and it's a great descriptor for this meal that brings together a lovely combination of tastes. A traditional Casado comprises rice, black beans, a salad, fried plantains, and a choice of meat such as chicken, beef, hog, or fish. I recall my first Casado encounter well. The platter was a brilliant rainbow of textures and flavours, each component matching the others flawlessly. The juicy grilled chicken, coupled with the savoury beans and the sweetness of the plantains, was a gourmet symphony. It's a meal that genuinely represents the spirit of Costa Rican home cuisine.

- **Sopa Negra**

On chilly days, I found consolation in a cup of Sopa Negra, or black bean soup. This substantial soup is prepared with black beans, onions, garlic, and cilantro, cooked to perfection. Often eaten with a hard-boiled egg and a dish of white rice, Sopa Negra is both healthy and tasty. I appreciated how the flavours mingled together, providing a rich and fulfilling supper. It's a meal that warms you from the inside out, great for those dreary days in the highlands.

- **Chifrijo**

One of my greatest discoveries was Chifrijo, a famous bar snack that rapidly became a particular favourite. This meal is a wonderful blend of rice, beans, chicharrón (crispy pork), and pico de gallo, all stacked in a bowl and topped with avocado and tortilla chips. The contrast of textures and tastes is absolutely enticing. I frequently loved Chifrijo with a nice drink, sitting at a neighbourhood tavern and taking in the colourful scene. It's a meal that's excellent for sharing with guests, each mouthful a blast of flavorful delight.

- **Olla de Carne**

For a taste of classic Costa Rican comfort cuisine, Olla de Carne is a must-try. This substantial beef stew is composed with pieces of meat, potatoes, carrots, yucca, and plantains, all cooked together in a savoury broth. The first time I encountered Olla de Carne, I was astounded by its depth of flavour. The juicy meat and the thick, aromatic broth were wonderfully gratifying. It's a meal that feels like a warm embrace, excellent for those days when you need a little extra comfort.

- **Arroz con Pollo**

Another iconic meal that I fell in love with is Arroz with Pollo, or chicken with rice. This bright meal is composed with rice, chicken, veggies, and a combination of spices, all cooked together in one pot. The outcome is a savoury and fragrant supper that's both soothing and tasty. I enjoyed how the rice absorbed all the flavours of the chicken and spices, producing a meal that's rich and fulfilling. It's a mainstay at family gatherings and festivities, and it's simple to understand why.

Exploring the native food of Costa Rica was a gourmet trip that I will always appreciate. Each meal tells a narrative, representing the rich cultural past and the kindness of the Costa Rican people. Whether you're savouring a robust breakfast of Gallo Pinto, a delicious lunch of Casado, or a soothing bowl of Sopa Negra, you're bound to fall in love with the tastes of Costa Rica.

International Cuisine Restaurants

Exploring the gastronomic scene of Costa Rica, I was happy to find a rich tapestry of foreign tastes that matched the native food nicely. From Italian trattorias to Japanese sushi bars, the range of different eateries offered a fascinating dimension to my culinary travels. Here are some of the remarkable spots that made a lasting effect on me.

La Baula Pizzeria

Address: Tamarindo, Guanacaste

One evening, desiring a bit of Italy, I strolled inside La Baula Pizzeria. The rustic appeal of the establishment, with its wood-fired oven and comfortable setting, quickly took me to a charming Italian town. I opted to sample their Margherita pizza, and it was a revelation. The crust was precisely thin and crunchy, topped with fresh tomatoes, mozzarella, and basil. The simplicity of the ingredients enabled each flavour to shine, making it one of the greatest pizzas I've ever eaten. The nice personnel and the bustling environment made it an ideal setting for a casual supper.

Bamboo Sushi Club

Address: Tamarindo, Guanacaste

For a flavour of Japan in the heart of Costa Rica, Bamboo Sushi Club is a must-visit. The clean, contemporary design and the quiet garden setting make a pleasant eating experience. I recall having the Dragon Roll, a wonderfully presented meal with fresh tuna, avocado, and a sprinkle of spicy mayo. Each mouthful was a wonderful blend of tastes and textures, demonstrating the chef's ability and attention to detail. The sushi was wonderfully fresh, and the presentation was nothing short of perfection. It was a pleasant retreat into the realm of Japanese food.

Dragonfly Thai Restaurant and Bar

Address: Tamarindo, Guanacaste

Craving some unique tastes, I found myself at Dragonfly Thai Restaurant and Bar. The vivid design and the enticing smells of Thai spices initially pulled me in. I went for Pad Thai, a traditional meal that did not disappoint. The noodles were properly cooked, with a lovely blend of shrimp, tofu, and crunchy peanuts, all mixed in a tangy tamarind sauce. The tastes were powerful and real, bringing me directly to the busy streets of Bangkok. The pleasant service and the vibrant environment made it a wonderful dinner experience.

El Chiringuito

Address: Playa Hermosa, Guanacaste

For a flavour of Spain, El Chiringuito is the place to be. This beachside restaurant has amazing views of the ocean, making it a wonderful setting for a leisurely dinner. I opted to taste their paella, a typical Spanish meal that was brimming with flavour. The saffron-infused rice was cooked to perfection, with large amounts of shrimp and a mix of veggies. The meal was thick and substantial, with each mouthful delivering a flavour of the Mediterranean. The relaxing mood and the sound of the waves made it an amazing eating experience.

Patagonia Argentinian Grill & Restaurant

Address: Tamarindo, Guanacaste

For a taste of Argentina, Patagonia Argentinian Grill & Restaurant is a jewel. The rich aromas of their grilled meats are just tempting. I recall loving their trademark steak, which was soft and juicy, cooked to perfection with their particular marinades. The warm and friendly ambiance, complemented with superb service, made it a dining experience to remember. They also provide a selection of vegetarian and seafood alternatives, ensuring there's something for everyone.

NOI Bistro

Address: Avenida Central Plaza, Tamarindo

For breakfast aficionados, NOI Bistro is a hidden treasure. This lovely café provides a great choice of breakfast dishes that will have you coming back for more. I really loved their EL NOI BF, which includes two eggs, fresh bread, hash browns, bacon, and Pico de Gallo. The quantities were big, and the tastes were right on. The relaxing environment and polite service made it a fantastic site to start my day before venturing out to explore Tamarindo.

Green Papaya Taco Bar

Address: Calle Central, Tamarindo

If you're in the mood for some tasty tacos, Green Papaya Taco Bar is the place to go. This lively eatery serves a variety of tacos, each overflowing with fresh ingredients and robust tastes. I adored the beef burrito, which was stuffed with delicious meat and topped with a tangy salsa. The bright design and laid-back feel made it a great location to hang out with friends. Their delicious margaritas were the ideal companion to the dinner, making it a very pleasurable dining experience.

Tamarindo's food culture is as broad and intriguing as its natural beauty. Each restaurant provides a distinct experience, reflecting the rich cultural fabric of this dynamic town. Whether you're a gourmet seeking for your next great meal or just someone who likes fine cuisine in a beautiful location, Tamarindo's dining scene is guaranteed to leave you satiated and wanting for more.

Chapter Five: TOP ATTRACTIONS

Beaches / Open / Close Hours (e.g., Manuel Antonio, Tamarindo)

Costa Rica's beaches are renowned, providing a combination of immaculate sands, crystal-clear seas, and teeming marine life. During my travels, I had the privilege of seeing some of the most magnificent beaches in Manuel Antonio and Tamarindo. Each beach has its own distinct charm and character, making every visit a wonderful experience. Here are some of the great beaches you should absolutely visit.

Manuel Antonio Beach

Open Hours: 7:00 AM - 4:00 PM (Tuesday to Sunday)

Manuel Antonio Beach, situated inside the Manuel Antonio National Park, is a piece of heaven. The first time I set foot on its silky, white beaches, I was amazed by the beauty of the turquoise seas and the thick flora around the beach. The beach is great for swimming, sunbathing, and even snorkelling. I spent hours exploring the gorgeous coral reefs close offshore, marvelling at the vivid fish and aquatic life. The beach is also an excellent site for animal viewing, with monkeys and iguanas regularly making an appearance. The park's well-maintained pathways make it simple to explore the neighbouring forest, providing an adventure flavour to your beach day.

Playa Espadilla

Open Hours: 7:00 AM - 4:00 PM (Tuesday to Sunday)

Just beyond the national park, Playa Espadilla provides a more laid-back beach experience. This huge beach is great for lengthy walks, with its broad expanse of sand and quiet waves. I enjoyed the easygoing feel here, with local merchants offering fresh coconuts and handcrafted items. The beach is also a popular area for surfing, and I couldn't resist getting a lesson from one of the kind local teachers. The waves were great for novices, and the joy of catching my first wave was memorable. As the sun sank, the sky changed into a painting of vivid hues, giving it the ideal finale to a great day.

Playa Biesanz

Open Hours: 7:00 AM - 4:00 PM (Tuesday to Sunday)

For a more isolated experience, Playa Biesanz is a hidden treasure. Tucked away in a little cove, this beach provides tranquil seas and a serene ambiance. I recall the sensation of serenity as I lounged on the smooth sand, listening to the soothing lapping of the waves. The beach is great for swimming and snorkelling, with clear seas that make it easy to view the rich marine life. The surrounding bush adds to the impression of remoteness, making it a wonderful site for a peaceful vacation.

Tamarindo Beach

Open Hours: 24 hours

Tamarindo Beach is a dynamic and busy location, noted for its boisterous atmosphere and outstanding surf. The beautiful beaches and mild waves make it popular among both residents and visitors. I spent many hours here, soaking in the sun and watching the surfers ride the waves. The beach is dotted with a variety of restaurants and bars, providing everything from fresh seafood to tropical drinks. One of my greatest memories is savouring a fantastic seafood platter at a beachside restaurant, with the sound of the waves providing the perfect backdrop. As night struck, the beach came alive with music and dancing, making it a terrific destination for nightlife as well.

Playa Langosta

Open Hours: 24 hours

Just south of Tamarindo, Playa Langosta provides a more quiet beach experience. This beach is famed for its magnificent sunsets and lovely tidal pools. I adored exploring the rocky beach, finding the various marine life in the tidal pools. The beach is also an excellent site for surfing, with waves that are appropriate for more experienced surfers. The quiet environment and natural beauty make it an ideal destination for a relaxed day by the shore.

Playa Avellanas

Open Hours: 24 hours

A short drive from Tamarindo, Playa Avellanas is a surfer's paradise. The beach is famed for its regular waves and laid-back ambiance. I adored seeing the surfers battle the waves, their talent and elegance a sight to behold. The beach is also home to Lola's, a renowned beachside restaurant named after a friendly pig that roams the shore. I couldn't resist ordering their famed fish tacos, which were as tasty as the scenery was spectacular. The mix of superb cuisine, nice people, and breathtaking surroundings makes Playa Avellanas one of my favourite destinations.

Exploring the beaches of Manuel Antonio and Tamarindo was a wonderful experience. Each beach provided something distinct, from the colourful marine life of Manuel Antonio to the boisterous surf culture of Tamarindo. Whether you're searching for adventure, leisure, or a little of both, these beaches are guaranteed to leave you with memorable memories.

National Parks and Wildlife Reserves (e.g., Tortuguero, Corcovado)

Costa Rica is a treasure trove of natural beauty, and its national parks and animal reserves are the crown jewels. During my travels, I had the honour of experiencing some of the most stunning and biodiverse locations in the nation. Here are a handful of my favourite national parks and wildlife reserves that you just must see.

- **Tortuguero National Park**

Tortuguero National Park, frequently referred to as the "Amazon of Costa Rica," is a location of exceptional beauty and variety. Accessible only by boat or air, the voyage to Tortuguero is an experience in itself. As I manoeuvred the meandering canals, surrounded by deep forest, I felt like I was entering a secret realm. The park is famed for its sea turtles, and I was fortunate enough to see the magnificent sight of a green sea turtle hatching on the beach. The park's network of rivers is great for exploration by kayak or canoe, giving a unique viewpoint on the lush rainforest and its residents. From colourful toucans to lively monkeys, the wildlife here is rich and varied. The peacefulness and natural beauty of Tortuguero made a lasting effect on me.

- **Corcovado National Park**

Dubbed "the most biologically intense place on Earth" by National Geographic, Corcovado National Park is a must-visit for every wildlife aficionado. Located on the secluded Osa Peninsula, this park is a refuge for animals and adventure. My voyage to Corcovado started with a fantastic boat ride down the coast, where I witnessed dolphins frolicking in the surf. Once inside the park, I was astounded by the sheer variety of life. Hiking through the deep jungle, I met everything from scarlet macaws and tapirs to the elusive jaguar. The park's gorgeous beaches are great for a refreshing dip after a day of walking. One of the highlights of my vacation was a guided night trek, when I observed the forest come alive with nocturnal wildlife. Corcovado's unspoiled environment and tremendous wildlife make it a really exceptional destination.

- **Monteverde Cloud Forest Reserve**

The Monteverde Cloud Forest Reserve is a strange and wonderful area, cloaked in mist and teaming with life. As I went along the woodland pathways, the chilly, wet air and the sound of pouring water created an ethereal mood.

The reserve is a haven for birdwatchers, with over 400 kinds of birds, including the dazzling quetzal. I was lucky enough to observe this secretive bird, its vivid plumage a striking contrast against the green greenery. The reserve's hanging bridges provide a unique view point, enabling you to wander amid the trees and enjoy the forest from a fresh perspective. The variety of plant life is remarkable, with innumerable types of orchids, ferns, and mosses. Monteverde's ethereal beauty and abundant biodiversity make it a must-visit location.

- **Manuel Antonio National Park**

Manuel Antonio National Park is a treasure on Costa Rica's Pacific coast, famed for its magnificent beaches and plentiful wildlife. The park's pathways weave through thick jungle, leading to stunning white-sand beaches that are great for swimming and snorkelling. I spent a beautiful day visiting the park, witnessing sloths leisurely hanging from trees and capuchin monkeys gleefully swinging through the canopy. The park's beaches are some of the most gorgeous I've ever seen, with crystal-clear seas and smooth, fluffy sand. One of the pleasures of my visit was a guided walk with a knowledgeable naturalist, who pointed out the park's unique flora and animals. Manuel Antonio's blend of natural beauty and fauna makes it a wonderful destination for nature enthusiasts.

- **Arenal Volcano National Park**

Arenal Volcano National Park is a stunning and awe-inspiring scenery, highlighted by the enormous Arenal Volcano. The park provides a variety of routes that lead you through lush rainforest, past bubbling hot springs, and to beautiful overlooks of the volcano. I was enthralled by the sight of the volcano, its beautiful cone soaring magnificently over the surrounding terrain.

The park is also home to a vast range of animals, including howler monkeys, toucans, and coatis. One of the highlights of my stay was a trek to the lava fields, where I could see the ruins of prior eruptions and feel the heat flowing from the earth. The park's hot springs are the ideal place to unwind after a day of trekking, with their warm, mineral-rich waters giving a pleasant bath. Arenal's spectacular landscape and geothermal marvels make it a must-visit location.

Exploring Costa Rica's national parks and animal reserves was a wonderful experience. Each park offers something distinct, from the peaceful canals of Tortuguero to the lush jungles of Corcovado. Whether you're a wildlife enthusiast, a birdwatcher, or just someone who loves nature, these parks are guaranteed to leave you with lasting memories and a profound appreciation for Costa Rica's natural splendour.

Hot Springs and Volcanoes (e.g., Arenal, Rincón de la Vieja)

Costa Rica's scenery is a monument to the sheer strength and beauty of nature, with its magnificent volcanoes and calming hot springs. During my travels, I got the chance to tour some of the most awe-inspiring volcanic zones and rest in the natural hot springs they generate. Here are some of the highlights from my trips.

- **Arenal Volcano and Hot Springs**

Arenal Volcano is one of Costa Rica's most famous monuments, and its presence is both intimidating and enchanting. The first time I saw Arenal, I was stunned by its magnificent conical form, soaring majestically over the verdant jungle. The volcano is still active, and although it hasn't erupted since 2010, the geothermal activity under the surface continues to heat the many hot springs in the vicinity.

One of my favourite experiences was basking in the hot springs at Tabacón Thermal Resort. The resort's natural hot springs are supplied by the geothermal waters of Arenal, producing a series of cascading pools surrounded by tropical gardens. The water was warm and pleasant, and I felt all my worry wash away as I sat in the mineral-rich waters. The backdrop was wonderful, with the sounds of the forest and the sight of the volcano in the background contributing to the tranquil ambiance.

Another wonderful site was EcoTermales, a more private hot spring experience. The pools here are smaller and less crowded, giving a pleasant respite. I enjoyed the rustic appeal of the location, with its natural stone ponds and rich flora. It was the ideal location to relax after a day of climbing around the volcano.

- **Rincón de la Vieja Volcano and Hot Springs**

Rincón de la Vieja is another volcanic marvel that provides a unique combination of adventure and tranquillity. The volcano is part of a bigger national park, which is a sanctuary for outdoor lovers. My journey to Rincón de la Vieja was full of excitement, as I explored the park's different landscapes, from deep woods to boiling mud pots and hot fumaroles.

One of the highlights of my vacation was trekking to the peak of the volcano. The trek was tough but rewarding, affording spectacular views of the surrounding countryside and the Pacific Ocean in the distance. The volcanic activity was obvious everywhere, with steam vents and hot springs dotting the landscape.

After a day of trekking, I treated myself to a visit to the Rio Negro Hot Springs. These hot springs are nestled along the banks of the Rio Negro River, and the location is truly wonderful. The pools are surrounded by beautiful woodland, and the murmur of the river adds to the serene mood. The water was pleasantly warm, and I felt revived as I swam in the natural pools. The hot springs also provide a unique volcanic mud bath experience, where you may cover yourself in mineral-rich mud before washing off in the hot springs. It was a fantastic and energetic way to conclude the day.

- **Miravalles Volcano and Hot Springs**

Miravalles Volcano, however less renowned than Arenal and Rincón de la Vieja, gives its own particular appeal. The volcano is situated in the Guanacaste province, and its geothermal activity has developed a multitude of hot springs and mud baths. My time in Miravalles was a great blend of rest and adventure.

One of the most unforgettable experiences was visiting the Las Hornillas Hot Springs. The hot springs are situated in a geothermal environment with boiling mud pots and steam vents. I liked resting in the warm waters, surrounded by the sights and sounds of geothermal activity. The highlight, however, was the volcanic mud bath. The mud was warm and velvety, and after covering myself in it, I felt my skin become extraordinarily soft and smooth. It was a wonderful and revitalising experience.

- **Poás Volcano**

Poás Volcano is one of Costa Rica's most accessible volcanoes, and its dynamic crater is a sight to see. The first time I glanced into the crater, I was amazed by the sheer scale and the beautiful blue hue of the acidic lake beneath. The volcano is situated in a national park, and the paths leading to the crater give beautiful views of the surrounding cloud forest.

While Poás doesn't have hot springs like Arenal or Rincón de la Vieja, its breathtaking terrain and the possibility to observe an active crater up close make it a must-visit site. The park also provides a variety of paths that lead you through lush woods and past spectacular waterfalls, giving a great combination of adventure and natural beauty.

Exploring Costa Rica's mountains and hot springs was a wonderful adventure. Each area gave its own distinct sensations, from the relaxing waters of Arenal's hot springs to the rough beauty of Rincón de la Vieja. Whether you're seeking adventure, leisure, or a little of both, Costa Rica's volcanic areas are guaranteed to leave you with lasting memories and a profound appreciation for the strength and beauty of nature.

Waterfalls and Adventure Parks

Costa Rica is a region of amazing natural treasures, and its waterfalls and adventure parks are among the most stimulating attractions. During my travels, I had the opportunity of experiencing some of the most spectacular waterfalls and exhilarating adventure parks the nation has to offer. Here are some of my top suggestions that you just must experience.

- **La Fortuna Waterfall**

Nestled amid the beautiful jungle near the Arenal Volcano, La Fortuna Waterfall is a sight to see. The first time I lay eyes on it, I was enthralled by the sheer strength and beauty of the flowing water. The waterfall plunges over seventy metres into a crystal-clear pool below, surrounded by colourful foliage. The journey down to the foot of the waterfall is a little steep, but the result is well worth the effort. I recall the delightful plunge I took in the chilly waters, feeling the spray from the cascade on my face. It's a fantastic site for a picnic, with lots of shady spaces to relax and enjoy the natural splendour.

- **Nauyaca Waterfalls**

Located in the southern area of Costa Rica, the Nauyaca Waterfalls are a hidden beauty. These twin waterfalls are among the most magnificent I've ever seen, with the larger falls tumbling over forty metres into a big lake, and the lower falls cascading into a smaller, more quiet pool. The trek to the waterfalls is an experience in itself, bringing you through lush forest and over rivers. I chose a horseback riding trip, which provided an additional dimension of adrenaline to the adventure. The sight of the waterfalls was stunning, and I couldn't resist having a plunge in the soothing waters. The natural beauty and quiet ambiance make Nauyaca Waterfalls a must-visit location.

- **Rio Celeste Waterfall**

The Rio Celeste Waterfall, situated in Tenorio Volcano National Park, is notable for its remarkable blue hue. According to local tradition, after God completed painting the sky, he dipped his paintbrush in the river, giving it its particular tint. The journey to the waterfall takes you through thick jungle, and the sight of the vivid blue water pouring into the pool below is simply breathtaking. Swimming is not permitted owing to the volcanic minerals in the water, but the scenery alone is worth the journey. I spent hours marvelling at the grandeur of the waterfall and exploring the surrounding trails, which give spectacular views of the park's rich flora and animals.

- **Montezuma Falls**

Montezuma Falls, situated on the Nicoya Peninsula, is a sequence of three waterfalls that provide a great combination of adventure and tranquillity. The climb to the falls is pretty short, and the reward is a sequence of tumbling waterfalls, each with its own particular appeal. The first waterfall is the highest, with a drop of nearly twenty metres into a large pool, suitable for swimming. The second and third waterfalls are smaller but as magnificent, with natural pools that are great for a refreshing plunge. I enjoyed the laid-back attitude of Montezuma and spent hours exploring the falls and lounging in the cold waters.

- **Adventure Park & Hotel Vista Golfo**

For those wanting an adrenaline thrill, Adventure Park & Hotel Vista Golfo is the place to go. Located in the heart of Costa Rica, this adventure park provides a choice of exhilarating sports, including zip-lining, rappelling, and high ropes courses. One of the highlights of my stay was the zip-line excursion, which takes you over eleven waterfalls, affording spectacular views of the surrounding area.

The sense of flying into the air, with the sound of falling water below, was amazing. The park also provides guided walks, horseback riding, and ATV trips, making it a fantastic location for adventure lovers.

- **Sky Adventures Monteverde Park**

Sky Adventures Monteverde Park is another must-visit for thrill-seekers. Located in the cloud forests of Monteverde, the park provides a range of activities that enable you to appreciate the splendour of the forest from above. The Sky Walk, a series of hanging bridges, gives stunning views of the forest canopy, while the Sky Tram takes you on a picturesque journey to the summit of the mountain. The highlight of my vacation was the Sky Trek zip-line tour, which provides a succession of high-speed zip-lines that transport you through the forest at incredible speeds. The mix of excitement and natural beauty makes Sky Adventures Monteverde Park a must-visit location.

- **Diamante Eco Adventure Park**

Diamante Eco Adventure Park, situated in Guanacaste, provides a unique combination of adventure and wildlife activities. The park's zip-line course is one of the longest in Costa Rica, affording breathtaking views of the Pacific Ocean and the surrounding jungle.

I adored the Superman zip-line, which enables you to soar face-first over the trees, affording a bird's-eye perspective of the countryside. The park also has a wildlife refuge, where you may witness a variety of species, including sloths, jaguars, and toucans. The mix of exhilarating activities and animal encounters makes Diamante Eco Adventure Park a wonderful destination for families and adventure fans alike.

Exploring Costa Rica's waterfalls and adventure parks was an incredible experience. Each place featured its own distinct combination of natural beauty and adventurous activities, making every visit a new experience. Whether you're seeking the calm of a hidden waterfall or the adrenaline rush of a zip-line tour, Costa Rica's waterfalls and adventure parks are guaranteed to leave you with lasting memories.

Popular Hikes & Walks (e.g., Monteverde Cloud Forest, Tenorio National Park)

Costa Rica's natural beauty is best enjoyed on foot, as every step unveils a new surprise. From misty cloud forests to vivid blue rivers, the country's various landscapes provide some of the most exciting climbs and excursions. Here are a couple of my favourite paths that you really must explore.

Monteverde Cloud Forest Reserve

The Monteverde Cloud Forest Reserve is a location where enchantment appears to linger in the air, very literally. The first time I visited the reserve, I was engulfed by a cold, foggy environment that seemed like walking into another universe. The paths here are well-maintained and provide a range of experiences, from simple walks to more strenuous excursions.

One of my favourite treks is the Sendero Bosque Nuboso, or Cloud Forest Trail. This track leads you deep into the heart of the forest, where the lush canopy above provides a mysterious environment. As I travelled, I marvelled at the vast variety, noticing everything from brilliant flowers to elusive quetzals. The highlight of the walk is the hanging bridge, which gives a beautiful view of the forest canopy. Walking amid the trees, with the mist whirling about, was an incredible experience.

Tenorio Volcano National Park

Tenorio Volcano National Park is home to one of Costa Rica's most spectacular natural wonders: the Rio Celeste. The river's vivid blue hue is the stuff of legends, and the journey to view it is as stunning. The trek to the Rio Celeste Waterfall is a fairly tough climb that takes you through beautiful jungle and past boiling hot springs.

The first time I saw Rio Celeste, I was amazed by its strange beauty. The water's deep blue tint is created by a unique chemical interaction between volcanic materials, producing a scene that looks almost unearthly. The trek to the waterfall is loaded with natural beauties, from the lush greenery to the sounds of exotic birds. The waterfall itself is a beautiful sight, with the blue water tumbling into a calm pool below. It's a trek that blends challenges with the pure beauty of nature.

Cerro Chirripó

For those wanting a more rigorous trip, Cerro Chirripó is the final challenge. As the tallest mountain in Costa Rica, reaching the top is no minor achievement, but the benefits are well worth the effort. The journey to the summit is a multi-day adventure that takes you through a range of environments, from tropical jungle to alpine tundra.

I recall the thrill of success I got when I reached the peak at daybreak. The view from the summit is nothing short of magnificent, with a vista that reaches from the Pacific Ocean to the Caribbean Sea. The trek is tough, but the sensation of seclusion and the breathtaking scenery make it a memorable experience. Along the route, I observed a vast assortment of species, from tapirs to hummingbirds, adding to the feeling of adventure.

Manuel Antonio National Park

Manuel Antonio National Park is not only recognized for its stunning beaches but also for its picturesque hiking routes. The park's paths provide a great combination of coastline vistas and thick rainforest, making it a hiker's delight. One of my favourite walks is the Punta Catedral Trail, which brings you to a spectacular vista overlooking the ocean.

The walk travels through the forest, where I encountered monkeys, sloths, and a variety of colourful birds. The highlight of the trek is the viewpoint at Punta Catedral, where the panoramic view of the coastline is just beautiful. The mix of rainforest and ocean vistas makes this climb a unique and gratifying experience.

Cahuita National Park

Cahuita National Park provides a more relaxing hiking experience, with a track that winds along the beach, affording spectacular views of the Caribbean Sea. The track is quite level and simple, making it suitable for a leisurely stroll.

I adored the laid-back attitude of Cahuita, with its gorgeous beaches and plentiful animals. The walk leads you through coastal rainforest and mangrove wetlands, where I encountered howler monkeys, sloths, and a variety of water birds. The highlight of the trek is the ability to swim in the crystal-clear waters of the Caribbean, making it a wonderful combination of hiking and beach time.

Rincón de la Vieja National Park

Rincón de la Vieja National Park is a hiker's delight, with a range of paths that take you through varied landscapes, from volcanic craters to lush woods. One of the most popular climbs is the Las Pailas Trail, which gives a fascinating insight into the park's geothermal activity.

The walk leads you past boiling mud pots, steaming fumaroles, and hot springs, creating a unique and surreal experience. I was interested by the geothermal characteristics, which are a monument to the park's volcanic beginnings. The walk also gives beautiful views of the surrounding environment, with the volcano towering in the background. It's a trek that blends adventure with the sheer force of nature.

Exploring Costa Rica's treks and walks was a voyage of discovery, each path having its own distinct combination of beauty and adventure. Whether you're seeking the mystical atmosphere of a cloud forest, the surreal beauty of a blue river, or the difficulty of ascending the highest mountain, Costa Rica's trails are guaranteed to leave you with lasting memories and a profound respect for the natural world.

Weather and Climate

Costa Rica's weather and temperature are as varied and interesting as its surroundings. From the sun-drenched beaches to the foggy cloud forests, the country's climate plays a crucial influence in defining its natural beauty and the experiences it provides. During my travels, I saw a variety of weather patterns that imparted a particular flavour to each site. Here's a thorough look at what you can anticipate while visiting this tropical paradise.

The Dry Season (December to April)

The dry season, called locally as "verano," is a favoured period for many vacationers. This time is marked by bright, rain-free days, making it excellent for beach vacations, hiking, and enjoying the outdoors. I recall my first visit to the Pacific coast during the dry season. The sky was a magnificent blue, and the sun shed a golden light over the sandy beaches. Temperatures varied from the mid-70s to the mid-90s Fahrenheit, giving great conditions for sunbathing and swimming sports.

One of the pleasures of visiting during the dry season is the quantity of animals. With less rain, animals are more readily noticed when they come out to bask in the sun or look for water. I experienced some of my finest wildlife interactions during this period, from watching monkeys play in the trees to seeing colourful birds in the jungle.

The Green Season (May to November)

The green season, or "invierno," provides a distinct type of splendour to Costa Rica. This time is defined by increasing rainfall, which changes the environment into a lush, brilliant green. The rain often occurs in the form of short afternoon downpours, leaving the mornings and evenings delightfully cool and clear. I thought the green season to be a lovely time to visit, with less visitors and a more calm vibe.

One of my fondest memories from the green season was trekking in the Monteverde Cloud Forest. The mist and rain imparted an ethereal character to the woodland, making it seem like a scene from a fairy tale. The paths were calmer, and the vegetation and animals looked even more colourful. The rain also brings out the finest in Costa Rica's waterfalls, which are at their most powerful and breathtaking during this season.

Microclimates and Regional Variations

Costa Rica's diverse geography generates a multitude of microclimates, each giving a distinct experience. The country's middle valley, where the capital San José is situated, offers a pleasant and temperate temperature year-round. I found the weather here to be refreshingly cool, with temps ranging from the mid-60s to the mid-70s Fahrenheit. This location is great for experiencing the city's cultural attractions and coffee plantations without the heat and humidity of the coast.

The Caribbean coast, on the other hand, is noted for its extreme humidity and frequent rains. This area gets rain throughout the year, with a small reprieve in September and October. I enjoyed the lush, tropical vibe of the Caribbean coast, with its deep jungles and lively fauna. The continual rain provides a beautiful, green environment that is great for nature enthusiasts.

The northern lowlands, home to the famed Arenal Volcano, see a combination of both dry and rainy seasons. The weather here may be erratic, with quick shifts from bright to wet. I found this location to be a mecca for adventure enthusiasts, with activities like hiking, zip-lining, and hot springs delivering a wonderful balance of thrill and relaxation.

Coastal Climates

The Pacific coast, including renowned resorts like Guanacaste and the Nicoya Peninsula, is noted for its warm and dry environment throughout the dry season. The beaches here are among the nicest in the nation, with golden sands and beautiful seas. I spent several afternoons lazing on the beach, enjoying the wonderful weather and spectacular sunsets.

The southern Pacific coast, including the Osa Peninsula, receives a more tropical climate with increased humidity and rainfall. This area is a biodiversity hotspot, and the jungles are filled with species. I found the weather here to be warm and humid, with periodic rain showers that contributed to the feeling of adventure.

Preparing for the Weather

When going to Costa Rica, it's vital to be prepared for the varied weather conditions. I always brought lightweight, breathable clothes for the hot and humid coastal areas, combined with a sturdy rain jacket and waterproof gear for the rainy season. Sturdy hiking boots were a requirement for exploring the trails, and I never forgot my sunscreen and bug protection.

Understanding Costa Rica's weather and temperature helped me make the most of my trip, enabling me to plan my activities and prepare properly. Whether you're basking in the sun on a Pacific beach, trekking through a foggy cloud forest, or exploring the lush rainforests of the Caribbean coast, Costa Rica's varied climate lends a new and rewarding depth to every journey.

Family-Friendly Activities / Open / Close Hours

Costa Rica is a delight for families, providing a multitude of activities that appeal to all ages. From exhilarating excursions to informative encounters, there's something for everyone. During my travels, I found a range of family-friendly sites that made our vacation unique. Here are some of the best activities that you and your family will adore.

Manuel Antonio National Park

Open Hours: 7:00 AM - 4:00 PM (Tuesday to Sunday)

Manuel Antonio National Park is a terrific place for families. The park's well-maintained pathways are great for tiny explorers, and the profusion of animals makes every trek an experience. I recall the thrill on my children's cheeks when they noticed their first sloth swinging lazily from a tree. The park's beaches are especially suitable for families, with calm seas perfect for swimming and snorkelling. We spent hours constructing sandcastles and looking for colourful fish in the shallow seas. The park's guided excursions are instructive and intriguing, giving unique insights into the native flora and animals.

La Paz Waterfall Gardens

Open Hours: 8:00 AM - 5:00 PM

La Paz Waterfall Gardens is a wonderful location that mixes natural beauty with educational displays. The gardens offer a number of magnificent waterfalls, grassy walkways, and a variety of animal displays. My kids were pleased to visit the butterfly observatory, where they could view hundreds of butterflies up close. The hummingbird garden was another pleasure, with these small birds darting about us as we strolled. The animal refuge is home to rescued species, including jaguars, monkeys, and toucans. It was a fantastic chance for my children to learn about conservation and the necessity of safeguarding animals.

Arenal Volcano National Park

Open Hours: 8:00 AM - 4:00 PM

A visit to Arenal Volcano National Park is a must for every family vacation to Costa Rica. The park provides a range of activities that appeal to all ages, from short treks to more strenuous paths. We took a guided trek to the lava fields, where we learnt about the volcano's history and the surrounding ecology. The park's hot springs were a success with the entire family, giving a pleasant way to conclude the day. The kids adored swimming in the warm, mineral-rich springs as we enjoyed the spectacular views of the volcano. The park also provides night excursions, which are a terrific chance to view the nocturnal creatures and the starry sky.

Monteverde Cloud Forest Reserve

Open Hours: 7:00 AM - 4:00 PM

The Monteverde Cloud Forest Reserve is a site of wonder and exploration. The reserve's hanging bridges give a unique view of the forest, enabling you to wander amid the trees. My children were thrilled with the different plant and animal life, from the brilliant orchids to the secretive quetzals. The reserve's guided excursions are both instructive and enjoyable, offering a greater knowledge of the cloud forest environment. We also visited the hummingbird exhibit, where hundreds of hummingbirds swarmed over us, producing a magnificent experience that we will never forget.

Tortuguero National Park

Open Hours: 6:00 AM - 6:00 PM

Tortuguero National Park is a unique place that provides a combination of adventure and education. The park is famed for its sea turtles, and we were fortunate enough to watch a turtle breeding on the beach. The guided boat rides through the park's canals were a highlight of our vacation, allowing a close-up look of the rich wildlife, including monkeys, caimans, and a variety of bird species. The park's visitor centre features interactive displays that are great for youngsters, delivering a fun and informative experience.

Diamante Eco Adventure Park

Open Hours: 8:30 AM - 4:30 PM

Diamante Eco excitement Park is a terrific venue for families seeking excitement. The park's zip-line course is one of the longest in Costa Rica, giving exhilarating rides with spectacular views of the Pacific Ocean. My kids liked the Superman zip-line, which enabled them to soar face-first over the trees. The park also contains a wildlife refuge, where we observed a variety of species, including sloths, jaguars, and toucans. The animal interactions were both enjoyable and instructive, bringing a better appreciation for Costa Rica's amazing biodiversity.

Palo Verde National Park

Open Hours: 8:00 AM - 4:00 PM

Palo Verde National Park is a birdwatcher's dream and a terrific trip for families. The park's marshes are home to a variety of bird species, and we enjoyed a guided boat excursion that brought us into the heart of the park. The youngsters were pleased to see crocodiles sunning on the riverbanks and monkeys swinging through the trees. The park's visitor centre features educational displays that give insights into the park's unique environment. It was a fantastic chance for the entire family to learn about the significance of wetlands and the species they sustain.

Exploring Costa Rica's family-friendly attractions was a fantastic experience. Each stop provided a distinct combination of adventure, knowledge, and natural beauty, making our vacation both entertaining and enlightening. Whether you're trekking through a cloud forest, relaxing in hot springs, or witnessing animals in a national park,

Costa Rica provides something for every member of the family.

Nearby Towns and Beaches

Costa Rica's beauty stretches well beyond its national parks and animal sanctuaries. The country's coastal cities and beaches provide a dynamic combination of culture, adventure, and leisure. Each village has its own distinct charm, making it a delight to explore. Here are some of the local towns and beaches that made a lasting effect on me.

Tamarindo

Tamarindo is a busy beach town on the Pacific coast, famed for its vibrant atmosphere and breathtaking sunsets. The first time I came to Tamarindo, I was captivated by the bright vitality of the city. The town is a sanctuary for surfers, with waves that appeal to both beginners and expert surfers. I decided to take a surf class, and the excitement of catching my first wave was memorable. The beach itself is gorgeous, with golden beaches and mild waves excellent for swimming. Tamarindo also provides a range of eating alternatives, from informal coastal cafés to expensive restaurants. One of my fondest memories is savouring a fresh seafood supper while watching the sun set over the water.

Jacó

Jacó is another renowned seaside town, noted for its active nightlife and adventurous activities. The town offers a laid-back feel throughout the day, with ample options for surfing, swimming, and sunbathing. I liked touring the adjacent Carara National Park, where I observed scarlet macaws and other unusual species. In the evening, Jacó comes alive with music and dancing, making it a perfect site to enjoy Costa Rica's dynamic nightlife. The town also provides a range of stores and marketplaces, excellent for picking up souvenirs and local crafts.

Montezuma

Montezuma is a hidden jewel on the Nicoya Peninsula, noted for its bohemian culture and magnificent natural beauty. The town is modest and laid-back, with a pleasant and inviting environment. I spent my days exploring the neighbouring waterfalls and hiking trails, and my nights resting at one of the town's numerous coastal cafés. The highlight of my stay was a boat cruise to Tortuga Island, where I snorkelled in crystal-clear seas and observed a variety of colourful fish and marine life. Montezuma's leisurely pace and natural beauty make it a wonderful location for anyone wishing to escape the rush and bustle of more touristic regions.

Puerto Viejo de Talamanca

Located on the Caribbean coast, Puerto Viejo de Talamanca provides a unique combination of Afro-Caribbean culture and gorgeous beaches. The town offers a laid-back, off-the-beaten-path air, with colourful architecture and a strong music culture.

I loved visiting the adjacent Cahuita National Park, where I climbed through beautiful jungle and snorkelling in the coral reefs. The town itself is full of charm, with a variety of eateries providing great Caribbean food. One of my favourite moments was savouring a meal of fresh seafood while listening to live reggae music.

Santa Teresa

Santa Teresa is a tiny seaside town on the Nicoya Peninsula, noted for its clean beaches and outstanding surf. The town offers a casual, bohemian air, with a mix of surfers, yogis, and tourists from across the globe. I spent my days surfing and doing yoga, and my nights enjoying the town's laid-back nightlife. The beach is lovely, with smooth white sand and clear blue waves. One of the highlights of my vacation was a sunset horseback ride down the beach, which was a genuinely spectacular experience.

Manuel Antonio

Manuel Antonio is a popular resort for its magnificent beaches and closeness to Manuel Antonio National Park. The town itself is tiny and attractive, with a variety of stores, restaurants, and cafés. I liked touring the park, where I observed a variety of species, including monkeys, sloths, and colourful birds. The beaches at Manuel Antonio are among the most gorgeous I've ever seen, with silky white sand and crystal-clear seas. I spent my days swimming, snorkelling, and resting on the beach, and my nights eating wonderful dinners at the town's various restaurants.

Nosara

Nosara is a quiet coastal town on the Nicoya Peninsula, noted for its yoga retreats and gorgeous beaches. The town offers a peaceful, laid-back attitude, with an emphasis on health and outdoor activities. I adored attending yoga lessons at one of the town's numerous studios, and visiting the neighbouring beaches and natural parks. The highlight of my stay was a guided tour of the Ostional Wildlife Refuge, where I observed hundreds of sea turtles breeding on the shore. Nosara's natural beauty and concentration on health make it a wonderful location for people wishing to rest and refresh.

Exploring Costa Rica's adjacent towns and beaches was a great experience. Each place had its own distinct combination of culture, adventure, and natural beauty, making every visit a new experience. Whether you're surfing in Tamarindo, partying the night away in Jacó, or resting on the gorgeous beaches of Nosara, Costa Rica's coastal towns are guaranteed to leave you with memorable memories.

Chapter Six: GETTING AROUND COSTA RICA

Renting Cars and Parking

Navigating the different landscapes of Costa Rica is an experience in itself, and renting a vehicle allows the opportunity to explore at your own speed. From the busy streets of San José to the isolated beaches of the Nicoya Peninsula, having your own car enables you to find hidden jewels and venture off the usual road. Here's a complete guide on renting vehicles and parking in Costa Rica, based on my own experiences.

Renting a Car

Renting a vehicle in Costa Rica is very uncomplicated, but there are a few things to keep in mind to guarantee a seamless experience. I recall the first time I hired a vehicle here; I was both thrilled and a little worried. The procedure starts with finding the correct rental business. While there are many worldwide brands accessible, I found that local firms frequently provide cheaper pricing and customised attention.

When hiring a vehicle, it's vital to plan in advance, particularly during the busy season. I opted for a 4x4 car, which proved helpful for negotiating the country's harsh terrain and gravel roads. The rental procedure normally involves a valid driver's licence, a credit card for the deposit, and proof of insurance. Costa Rica requires third-party liability insurance, which is generally included in the rental quotation, but it's good to double-check to prevent any surprises.

One advice I found beneficial is to properly check the vehicle before driving off. Take note of any existing damage and ensure it's recorded by the rental provider. This might prevent you from any conflicts while returning the automobile. Also, educate yourself with the local driving regulations and road signs, since they might vary from what you're accustomed to.

Driving in Costa Rica

Driving in Costa Rica is an experience, with its own set of difficulties and pleasures. The country's road network is usually adequate, although certain locations, particularly rural ones, may be challenging to manage. I immediately learnt that patience and prudence are crucial. The major highways are well-maintained, but minor roads may be narrow and meandering, frequently with unforeseen impediments like potholes or cattle.

One of the benefits of driving in Costa Rica is the gorgeous landscape. From the lush jungles to the dramatic coasts, every route provides stunning sights. I really appreciated the journey from San José to the Arenal Volcano, where the environment transforms from urban sprawl to lush hills and lovely communities.

Parking

Parking in Costa Rica varies based on the area. In metropolitan places like San José, obtaining a parking space may be tough, particularly during peak hours. I found that utilising paid parking lots or garages was the safest alternative. These facilities are generally safe and conveniently positioned near major attractions and retail districts.

In smaller cities and seaside resorts, parking is often more lenient. Many hotels and restaurants provide free parking for visitors. However, it's always a good idea to check for any parking restrictions or signs indicating no-parking zones. I recall parked near Manuel Antonio National Park, where local personnel volunteered to look after the vehicle for a modest price. While this isn't essential, it may bring peace of mind.

Safety Tips

Safety is crucial while driving and parking in Costa Rica. Here are a few suggestions I found helpful:

1. Avoid leaving valuables in the car: This is a basic rule of thumb, but it's particularly vital in tourist regions. I always made care to take my valuables with me or stow them out of sight in the trunk.

2. Use well-lit and safe parking areas: Especially in metropolitan locations, choose for parking lots with security guards or surveillance cameras.

3. Be careful of road conditions: Weather may change swiftly, impacting road conditions. During the rainy season, certain roadways might become slick or flooded. I always checked the weather forecast and road conditions before starting out on lengthy travels.

4. Stay alert: Costa Rican driving may be erratic, and traffic signs may not always be apparent. Staying vigilant and driving conservatively helped me travel safely.

Exploring Off the Beaten Path

One of the biggest benefits of hiring a vehicle is the chance to go off the main road. Some of my most memorable encounters in Costa Rica were in distant regions that are difficult to access by public transit. For instance, the trip to Monteverde Cloud Forest Reserve brought me via winding mountain roads with beautiful vistas. The ability to stop and soak in the landscape, explore little communities, and uncover secret waterfalls made the experience very unique.

Another pleasure was travelling around the Nicoya Peninsula, where I encountered isolated beaches and wonderful coastal communities. The freedom of owning a vehicle enabled me to explore at my own leisure, stopping whenever anything grabbed my attention.

Renting a vehicle in Costa Rica offers up a world of options, enabling you to enjoy the country's natural beauty and lively culture on your own terms. With a little planning and a spirit of adventure, you'll discover that navigating Costa Rica by automobile is an enriching and fascinating experience.

Domestic Flights and Shuttle Services

Travelling around Costa Rica is an experience in itself, and although hiring a vehicle gives freedom, sometimes the ease of domestic flights and shuttle services is unsurpassed. During my trips, I learned that these alternatives not only save time but also present distinct vistas of the country's different landscapes. Here's a thorough look at how to make the most of domestic flights and shuttle services in Costa Rica.

Domestic Flights

Flying domestically in Costa Rica is a terrific option to traverse big distances fast, particularly if you're short on time or want to avoid the occasionally tough road conditions. I recall my first domestic flight with SANSA Airlines, which flies out of San

José. The trip was seamless and efficient, and the sights from the aircraft were nothing short of magnificent. Watching the verdant jungles, flowing rivers, and clean beaches from above gave me a new respect for the country's natural splendour.

SANSA and Costa Rica Green Airways are the primary domestic airlines, providing flights to famous places including Tamarindo, Quepos, and Puerto Jiménez. The flights are quite short, typically around an hour, making it convenient to jump from one location to another. I found the scheduling procedure uncomplicated, and the tiny aircraft gave a more intimate and personal flying experience. One suggestion I picked up is to travel light, since the luggage limitations on local flights are more stringent than foreign flights.

Shuttle Services

For those who want to remain grounded, shuttle services are an ideal option. Costa Rica's shuttle network is vast, linking major towns, tourist spots, and even isolated places. I typically utilised shared shuttles for their price and convenience. These shuttles are generally contemporary, air-conditioned vehicles that give a pleasant journey. One of my favourite shuttle trips was riding from San José to La Fortuna. The tour was picturesque, and the driver was knowledgeable, offering fascinating details about the regions we travelled through.

Private shuttles are another fantastic alternative, particularly for families or parties. They provide the opportunity to create your own timetable and make stops along the road. I recall hiring a private shuttle for a vacation to Monteverde. The driver was courteous, enabling us to stop for photographs and even a brief bite at a local bakery. The customised care made the travel delightful and stress-free.

Combining Flights and Shuttles

One of the greatest methods to enhance your travel experience in Costa Rica is to combine domestic flights with shuttle services. This technique enables you to travel big distances fast by plane and then explore smaller places more completely by driving. For example, I flew from San José to Puerto Jiménez and then took a shuttle to my resort on the Osa Peninsula. This combo saved me hours of travel time and enabled me to enjoy the gorgeous trip through the jungle.

Practical Tips

When organising your journey, it's vital to consider a few practical guidelines to guarantee a seamless experience. For domestic flights, always check the luggage rules and arrive at the airport at least an hour before departure. The smaller airports may be pretty efficient, but it's always preferable to have some additional time.

For shuttle services, scheduling in advance is essential, particularly during the hot season. I noticed that most shuttle providers offer online reservations, making it simple to reserve your position. It's also a good idea to confirm your pick-up time and location a day before your trip. The drivers are normally prompt, however having a contact number accessible might be beneficial in case of any changes.

Enjoying the Journey

One of the attractions of visiting Costa Rica is the adventure itself. Whether you're flying over the trees in a tiny aircraft or meandering along mountain roads in a shuttle, each method of travel provides its own distinct sensations. I enjoyed the feeling of adventure that came with each journey, from the suspense of departure to the pleasure of seeing animals along the way.

Travelling via domestic flights and shuttle services in Costa Rica opened me a world of options, enabling me to see the country's different areas with ease. Whether you're wanting to save time, enjoy beautiful roads, or just experience a new way of getting about, these alternatives give a convenient and fun way to explore everything that Costa Rica has to offer.

Public Bus Services

Navigating Costa Rica by public bus is an experience that gives a unique view into the everyday life of the nation. The brilliant colours of the buses, the lively discussions among passengers, and the ever-changing landscape make every voyage unique. Here's a thorough look at how to make the most of Costa Rica's enormous public bus network, based on my own experiences.

The Charm of Public Buses

One of the first things I noticed about Costa Rica's public buses is its attractiveness. Each bus is a microcosm of Costa Rican culture, packed with natives and foreigners alike. The buses are generally brilliantly painted, with colourful graphics that represent the country's exuberant character. I recall boarding a bus in San José, where the driver welcomed me with a warm grin and a welcoming "Pura Vida!" The spirit of togetherness and kindness was evident, making me feel immediately welcome.

Extensive Network

Costa Rica's public bus network is enormous, spanning practically every part of the nation. From busy cities to isolated villages, there's a bus that can transport you there. I found the buses to be a trustworthy and economical method to travel, particularly for longer distances. The primary centre for bus travel is San José, where various terminals service diverse districts. Navigating the terminals may be a little stressful at first, but I soon got the knack of it with a little assistance from the locals.

Planning Your Journey

Planning a bus trip in Costa Rica involves a little study, but it's definitely worth the effort. I utilised web tools and local guidance to find out the best routes and timetables.

One suggestion I found essential was to continually check the newest timetables, since they might change regularly. The bus companies regularly publish timetables at the terminals, and I established a practice of snapping a snapshot of the schedule board for reference.

The Experience

Riding the bus in Costa Rica is an event in itself. The buses are normally pleasant, with cushioned seats and huge windows that give fantastic views of the passing countryside. I liked seeing the scenery change as we moved from the city to the countryside.

The buses might become full, particularly during peak hours, but this simply contributed to the feeling of adventure. I regularly began up talks with other passengers, who were always willing to give insights and experiences about their trips.

Cost and Convenience

One of the major benefits of utilising public buses in Costa Rica is the cost. The rates are relatively inexpensive, making it a perfect alternative for budget travellers. I was pleasantly astonished at how far I could go for only a few colones. The buses also run often, particularly on busy routes, so I never had to wait long for the next one.

Safety and Comfort

Safety and comfort are crucial factors while travelling by bus. I found the buses to be mostly safe, although it's always important to keep a check on your possessions, particularly in busy locations. I took caution to keep my valuables nearby and placed a little lock on my bag for further protection. The buses are normally clean and well-maintained, with some even having amenities like air conditioning and Wi-Fi.

Scenic Routes

Some of the most gorgeous roads in Costa Rica may be enjoyed by bus. One of my favourite travels was from San José to Monteverde. The meandering roads carried us past lush woods and undulating hills, with spectacular vistas at every turn. Another memorable excursion was the travel down the Pacific coast to Manuel Antonio, where the bus followed the beach, affording spectacular ocean vistas.

Local Insights

Travelling by bus also provided me with a greater insight into local life. I loved witnessing the everyday activities of the passengers, from school children in their uniforms to farmers headed to the market. The bus stops in tiny towns and villages provided a terrific chance to visit off-the-beaten-path sites. I regularly jumped off the bus to explore local markets, taste traditional delicacies, and interact with the inhabitants.

Practical Tips

Here are a few practical recommendations for making the most of your bus trip in Costa Rica:

1. Carry tiny Change: Bus fares are normally paid in cash, and carrying tiny change makes the procedure simpler.

2. Pack Light: Buses may become packed, so it's better to go with a small bag or backpack.
3. Stay Hydrated: Bring a water bottle, particularly for longer flights.
4. Be Patient: Schedules may be flexible, and delays are not unusual. Embrace the slow pace and enjoy the adventure.

Travelling by public bus in Costa Rica was an amazing experience that enabled me to explore the nation from a new perspective. The price, convenience, and chance to engage with people made it one of my favourite ways to travel about. Whether you're travelling to a famous tourist attraction or discovering a hidden treasure, the public bus system provides a dependable and entertaining way to see Costa Rica.

Taxi and Ride-Sharing Options

Navigating the bustling streets and picturesque pathways of Costa Rica is an experience that may be made even easier with the use of taxis and ride-sharing services. Whether you're touring the busy metropolis of San José or driving to a distant beach, these alternatives give flexibility and simplicity. Here's a thorough look at my experiences using taxis and ride-sharing in Costa Rica.

The Ubiquitous Red Taxis

One of the first things you'll notice in Costa Rica are the red taxis with their trademark yellow triangles. These licensed taxis are a regular sight and a trustworthy source of transportation.

My first journey in a red cab was from the airport to my hotel in San José. The driver was courteous and knowledgeable, providing advice on local sites and places to dine. The cabs are metered, which assures fair pricing, and I found the charges to be acceptable.

Official cabs are regulated and must conform to particular criteria, which provided me with a peace of mind about safety and trustworthiness. I immediately learned to check for the yellow triangle and the official licence plate to verify I was getting into a real cab. The drivers are generally locals who know the region well, giving them a terrific resource for insider information and suggestions.

Airport Taxis

When arriving at either of Costa Rica's two airports, Juan Santamaría International Airport in San José or Daniel Oduber Quirós International Airport in Liberia, you'll find a fleet of orange cabs waiting outside. These cabs are particularly intended for airport trips and are significantly more costly than the red ones. My experience with the airport cabs was easy and efficient. The drivers were competent and assisted with my bags, making the transfer from the airport to my location hassle-free.

Ride-Sharing Services

Ride-sharing services like Uber have been more popular in Costa Rica, particularly in metropolitan areas. I found Uber to be a useful alternative, especially in San José and other big cities. The app operates exactly like it does in other countries, enabling you to order a trip, check the fee estimate, and monitor your driver's arrival. One of the benefits of utilising Uber is the option to pay using the app, which removes the need for cash transactions.

My first Uber trip in Costa Rica was from my hotel in San José to a restaurant across town. The driver came immediately, and the vehicle was clean and comfy. We had a good talk about the city, and I enjoyed the ease of being dropped off directly at the restaurant's door. Uber also gives the ability to rate your driver, which helps maintain a high quality of service.

Safety and Convenience

Safety is always a consideration while travelling, and I found both taxis and ride-sharing services in Costa Rica to be relatively safe. However, it's always prudent to take a few precautions. For taxis, I took care to remember the taxi number and the driver's name, which are normally posted inside the vehicle. For ride-sharing, I confirmed the driver's information and the car's licence plate before getting in.

One of the perks of utilising these services is the option to travel at any time of day or night. This was especially beneficial when I had early morning flights or late-night landings. The availability of taxis and ride-sharing services around the clock assured me that I could travel to my location securely and without fuss.

Exploring Beyond the Cities

While taxis and ride-sharing services are easily accessible in metropolitan areas, they may also be utilised to visit sites outside the cities. I once took a cab from San José to the adjacent town of Cartago to see the famed Basilica of Our Lady of the Angels. The driver was eager to wait while I visited the basilica and even recommended a few other local places to see.

For longer travels, it's feasible to arrange a fixed charge with the taxi driver. This might be a cost-effective solution for day trips or excursions to regions where public transit could be restricted. I found the drivers to be courteous and eager to adjust the tour to my interests.

Practical Tips

Here are a few practical suggestions for utilising taxis and ride-sharing services in Costa Rica:

1. Carry tiny notes: While most cabs take cash, it's nice to carry tiny notes for quicker transactions.
2. Use the App: For ride-sharing, utilising the app guarantees you receive a fair fee and can monitor your journey.

3. Confirm the fee: For lengthier taxi journeys, confirm the fee with the driver before beginning the journey.

4. remain Connected: Having a local SIM card or access to Wi-Fi makes it simpler to utilise ride-sharing applications and remain in contact.

Navigating Costa Rica using taxis and ride-sharing services brought a dimension of ease and flexibility to my visits. Whether I was headed to a secluded beach, experiencing a new city, or just commuting from the airport to my hotel, these alternatives offered dependable and pleasant transportation. The pleasant drivers and the convenience of use made moving about Costa Rica a pleasure, enabling me to concentrate on enjoying the ride and exploring everything that this lovely nation has to offer.

Chapter Seven: PRACTICAL INFORMATION

Tourist Information Offices (Locations, Hours, Services)

Exploring a new country may be both fascinating and a little scary, but Costa Rica's tourist information centres are a terrific resource to help you get the most out of your vacation. During my travels, I found these offices to be quite useful, giving anything from maps and brochures to customised counsel. Here's a thorough look at the locations, hours, and services offered by Costa Rica's tourist information offices.

San José - Juan Santamaría International Airport

One of my first visits upon landing in Costa Rica was the tourist information centre at Juan Santamaría International Airport. Located directly in the arrivals hall, this office is a fantastic spot to regain your bearings. The personnel were really helpful and offered me maps, brochures, and a lot of information about area activities and transit alternatives. The office is open from early morning until late evening, guaranteeing that passengers coming at diverse hours may obtain the service they need. Their advice in navigating San José and suggestions for local motels were extremely useful.

San José - Downtown

In the centre of San José, the major tourist information office is located near the National Theatre. This strategically placed office is a terrific resource for discovering the city's cultural and historical treasures. Open from 8:00 AM to 5:00 PM, Monday through Saturday, the office provides services such as guided tour reservations, event information, and extensive maps of the city. I recall dropping here to ask directions to the Jade Museum and ended up conversing with the staff about the finest local restaurants. Their intimate advice led me to some wonderful eating experiences that I may have otherwise missed.

Liberia - Daniel Oduber Quirós International Airport

For travellers coming in the Guanacaste area, the tourist information office at Daniel Oduber Quirós International Airport in Liberia is a must-visit. This office is conveniently placed in the arrivals area and is open from 7:00 AM to 9:00 PM. The staff supplied me with thorough information on the region's beaches, national parks, and adventure activities. They also helped me organise transportation to my hotel, making my arrival stress-free. The pamphlets and maps I picked up here were useful for organising my trips to destinations like Rincon de la Vieja National Park and the lovely beaches of Playa Hermosa.

La Fortuna

La Fortuna, recognized for its closeness to Arenal Volcano, features a well-equipped tourist information office situated in the town centre. Open daily from 8:00 AM to 6:00 PM, this office provides a variety of services including tour reservations, transportation arrangements, and information on nearby attractions. I found their advice on trekking paths and thermal springs extremely beneficial. The personnel were educated about the ideal times to see the volcano and the other activities offered in the vicinity. Their ideas helped me make the most of my stay in La Fortuna, from zip-lining experiences to resting in the hot springs.

Monteverde

In the cloud forest area of Monteverde, the tourist information office is a crucial resource for travellers. Located near the major bus station in Santa Elena, the office is open from 8:00 AM to 5:00 PM. The personnel here gave me thorough maps of the hiking paths and information on the many reserves in the region. They also gave suggestions on birding and the best sites to observe the elusive quetzal. I liked their instruction on the many canopy tours and hanging bridges, which made my investigation of the cloud forest even more memorable.

Manuel Antonio

Manuel Antonio's tourist information centre is conveniently positioned near the entrance to Manuel Antonio National Park. Open from 7:00 AM to 4:00 PM, our office is a fantastic starting place for exploring the park and its surroundings. The staff offered me maps of the park's trails, information on guided tours, and suggestions on the ideal times to visit the beaches to avoid the crowds. Their recommendations on nearby eateries and lodgings was also quite useful. I found their passion for the region contagious, and their suggestions lead to some wonderful experiences, including a guided night trip where I observed a variety of nocturnal creatures.

Tamarindo

In the busy seaside resort of Tamarindo, the tourist information office is located in the town centre, near to the major beach. Open from 9:00 AM to 6:00 PM, this office provides a variety of services including surf instruction reservations, information on local events, and suggestions for food and entertainment. The personnel were pleasant and educated, offering me with recommendations on the finest surf places and the safest bathing sites. Their recommendations on local activities, such as boat rides to view dolphins and snorkelling excursions, helped me make the most of my stay in Tamarindo.

Visiting Costa Rica's tourist information centres was a crucial aspect of my vacation experience. Each office offered great tools and individual counsel that enriched my trip. Whether you're seeking for maps, tour reservations, or insider information, these offices are available to help you make the most of your stay in this lovely nation.

Essential Maps: Navigating the Country and Major Attractions

SCAN THE QR CODE
1. Open your phone's camera.
2. Point it at the QR code.
3. Wait for it to focus.
4. Once recognized, tap the notification.
5. Follow the link or information provided.

Arenal Volcano National Park

SCAN THE QR CODE

1. Open your phone's camera.
2. Point it at the QR code.
3. Wait for it to focus.
4. Once recognized, tap the notification.
5. Follow the link or information provided.

SAN JOSE

SCAN THE QR CODE

1. Open your phone's camera.
2. Point it at the QR code.
3. Wait for it to focus.
4. Once recognized, tap the notification.
5. Follow the link or information provided.

MANUEL ANTONIO BEACH

Currency, Language, Safety, and Local Customs

When I first set foot in Costa Rica, I was instantly taken by the colourful culture and the great friendliness of its people. However, to completely immerse myself in the experience, I needed to comprehend certain practical elements of everyday living. Here's a full look at the currency, language, safety precautions, and local traditions that helped me explore this lovely nation.

Currency

Costa Rica uses the Costa Rican colón, abbreviated as CRC. The bright banknotes, decorated with photos of the country's abundant fauna, were a treat to hold. I immediately realised that although US dollars are often accepted, particularly in tourist areas, having colones on hand makes transactions easier and often more inexpensive. I found it easy to convert money at banks and official exchange offices, avoiding the less advantageous rates at airports and hotels.

One of my first lessons was to acquaint oneself with the denominations. The banknotes come in different colours and sizes, making them easier to detect. Coins, ranging from 5 to 500 colones, are also regularly used. I made sure to pack tiny dollars and coins for regular transactions, since bigger bills may often be difficult to break in smaller businesses and rural locations.

Language

Spanish is the official language of Costa Rica, and although many people in tourist regions speak English, I found that learning a few basic Spanish words dramatically boosted my interactions with locals. Costa Rican Spanish, or "Tico Spanish," has its own distinctive idioms and terminology. For instance, "Pura Vida" is a term you'll hear frequently, representing the country's laid-back and optimistic view on life. It might imply anything from "hello" and "goodbye" to "everything's great."

In addition to Spanish, there are various indigenous languages spoken by the local people, such as Bribri and Cabécar. While I didn't encounter these languages much, knowing about them offered richness to my knowledge of Costa Rica's cultural variety.

Safety

Costa Rica is typically a safe place to visit, but like any vacation, it's necessary to be vigilant and take measures. Petty theft may be a concern, especially in busy settings and on public transit. I made it a practice to keep my possessions safe and avoid flaunting valuables. Using a money belt or a safe bag made me feel more at peace.

When travelling places, I was watchful, particularly at night. Sticking to well-lit and crowded locations was a wise habit. In rural and distant locations, I found the residents to be really nice and helpful, although it's always important to let someone know your intentions if you're headed off the main route.

One safety suggestion that stuck out was to be careful with drinking at pubs and clubs. There have been allegations of beverages being tainted, so I constantly kept an eye on my beverage and avoided taking drinks from strangers.

Local Customs

Understanding local norms was crucial to feeling at home in Costa Rica. The people, known as Ticos, are recognized for their civility and regard for others. Greetings are warm and typically feature a brief kiss on the cheek, particularly among friends and relatives. In more formal circumstances, a handshake is acceptable.

Costa Ricans regard timeliness differently than in some other cultures. "Tico time" is a laid back attitude to scheduling, where being a little late is typically accepted. This took some getting used to, but I learned to accept the slower pace and enjoy the moment.

Dress rules in Costa Rica are largely informal, however modesty is encouraged, particularly in rural regions and religious locations. I thought it appropriate to dress modestly while visiting churches or attending local activities.

Environmental sensitivity is another essential component of Costa Rican society. The nation is a leader in ecotourism and conservation activities. I took cautious to meet municipal requirements for garbage disposal and participated in recycling programs wherever feasible. Respecting animals and natural environments was also a priority, since Costa Ricans take great pleasure in their country's biodiversity.

My experience in Costa Rica was boosted by learning these practical factors. The money, language, safety precautions, and local traditions all played a part in making my vacation simple and pleasurable. Embracing these qualities helped me to connect more closely with the nation and its people, making my experience really unique.

Chapter Eight:
NEIGHBOURING TOWNS & REGIONS

San José

The early air in San José holds a special combination of freshness and expectancy, as if the city itself is anxious to disclose its secrets with those prepared to investigate. As I walked out of my hotel, the lively energy of Costa Rica's capital surrounded me, promising a day packed with exploration and adventure. San José, frequently considered as only a portal to the country's natural treasures, proved itself to be a treasure mine of cultural and historical jewels, each waiting to be unearthed.

My first trip was to the renowned National Theatre, a symbol of elegance and artistic legacy. Walking through its majestic entryway, I was instantly impressed by the luxury of its interior. The ceilings, covered with beautiful paintings, and the marble sculptures that lined the corridors, spoke of a bygone period of grandeur. It was easy to envisage the innumerable acts that have graced its stage, each one contributing to the rich fabric of Costa Rican culture.

Next, I headed into the centre of the city to investigate the Central Market. This crowded bazaar was a sensory joy, with its tiny lanes overflowing with bright shops. The perfume of freshly ground coffee blended with the flavour of tropical fruits, producing an enticing mixture that was distinctly San José. I spent hours roaming around the market, eating local delicacies and participating in spirited discussions with the merchants, each one eager to share a bit of their culture with me.

San José's museums gave an interesting peek into the country's history. The Pre-Columbian Gold Museum, with its enormous collection of ancient artefacts, took me back to the period of Costa Rica's early civilizations. Each object, from elaborately carved jewellery to ceremonial masks, revealed a tale of a rich and colourful society that had lived long before the advent of Europeans. The Jade Museum, devoted to preserving the past of Costa Rica's indigenous peoples, was equally compelling. The exhibitions showed the beauty and importance of jade in local customs, offering a greater knowledge of the cultural history that continues to define the country.

One of the most charming characteristics of San José was its bustling street life. The Avenida Central, a busy pedestrian boulevard, was usually abuzz with activity. Street entertainers delighted visitors with music and dancing, while painters showcased their crafts in spontaneous galleries. The enthusiasm was intoxicating, and I frequently found myself pulled to the bustling environment, where the soul of the city was on full show.

San José's natural grounds offered a quiet getaway from the metropolitan buzz. La Sabana Metropolitan Park, widely referred to as the "lungs of San José," was a refuge of peace. I spent a relaxing day meandering across its spacious grounds, enjoying the sight of families picnicking and children playing. The park also hosted the Costa Rican Art Museum, where I found a wonderful collection of artworks that highlighted the country's unique cultural legacy.

As my stay in San José drew to a conclusion, I realised that this city had provided me with a microcosm of Costa Rica itself. It is a location where history and modernity live peacefully, where the past is cherished, and the future is accepted. The experiences I formed here, from the busy markets to the quiet parks, will long remind me of the dynamic character of San José.

Leaving San José was bittersweet. While I was anxious to experience more of Costa Rica's natural treasures, I knew that this city had left an unforgettable impact on my heart. San José is more than simply a gateway to the country's famous beaches and rainforests; it is a destination in its own right, replete with culture, history, and an irresistible charm. As I boarded the bus to my next journey, I took with me the spirit of San José, a city that had welcomed me with open arms and given its soul.

Liberia

The early morning light gave a warm glow over the picturesque town of Liberia, and as I went out into the cobblestone streets, I felt a feeling of exhilaration and wonder. Liberia, popularly referred to as the "White City" because of its whitewashed colonial structures, is a gateway to some of Costa Rica's most breathtaking natural beauties. Nestled in the Guanacaste region, this town has a combination of rich history, lively culture, and stunning views.

My first visit was to the ancient core of Liberia, where the colonial architecture took me back in time. The Iglesia Inmaculada Concepción de María, with its stunning white façade, stood brightly in the town plaza. As I entered the church, the cold, quiet interior created a dramatic contrast to the busy streets outside. The beautiful woodwork and stained glass windows were a monument to the town's rich cultural past.

Wandering around the streets, I came across the Museo de Guanacaste, built in a former military barracks. The museum offers an interesting view into the region's history, from pre-Columbian periods to the current day. The displays exhibited everything from ancient antiquities to current art, presenting a thorough account of Guanacaste's cultural development. I was especially attracted by the tales of the indigenous Chorotega people, whose history continues to impact the area.

Liberia's lively marketplaces were another pleasure of my vacation. The Mercado Central was a sensory joy, with its bright kiosks loaded with fresh fruit, homemade crafts, and local delights. I couldn't resist eating some of the traditional meals, including gallo pinto and tamales, which were brimming with flavour. The affable merchants were eager to impart their culinary secrets, and I departed with a renewed respect for Costa Rican food.

One of the most captivating qualities of Liberia is its closeness to some of Costa Rica's most stunning natural wonders. Just a short drive from the town, I found myself at the entrance of Rincón de la Vieja National Park. The park, named for the active volcano that dominates its environment, is a paradise for outdoor lovers. I spent the day wandering through lush woods, past boiling mud pots and scorching fumaroles, marvelling at the sheer majesty of nature. The highlight of my vacation was a plunge in the natural hot springs, where the warm, mineral-rich waters gave the ideal rest after a full day of sightseeing.

Another local wonder is the magnificent Llanos de Cortés waterfall. Tucked deep in a quiet woodland, this waterfall is a truly hidden gem. As I neared, the sound of falling water got louder, and the sight of the falls, with their crystal-clear pool at the foot, stole my breath away. I spent a beautiful day swimming in the calm waves and reclining on the sandy coast, surrounded by the beauty of nature.

Liberia is also a gateway to the magnificent beaches of the Pacific coast. Playa Hermosa, with its golden sands and calm surf, was the ideal site for leisure. I spent my days here soaking in the sun, snorkelling in the lovely seas, and enjoying the laid-back vibe of the beachfront eateries. The sunsets were especially magnificent, painting the sky in shades of orange and pink, and bringing a great finale to each day.

As my stay in Liberia drew to a conclusion, I pondered on the various things that had made my journey so unforgettable. From the rich history and colourful culture to the gorgeous natural settings, Liberia has given a great combination of adventure and leisure. This wonderful village, with its kind and inviting inhabitants, had captivated my heart, and I knew that the memories I formed here would remain with me forever.

Leaving Liberia was bittersweet. While I was delighted to continue my adventure across Costa Rica, I knew that this place had left an unforgettable impact on my spirit. Liberia is more than simply a gateway to the delights of Guanacaste; it is a destination in its own right, replete with history, culture, and natural beauty. As I boarded the bus to my next adventure, I took with me the soul of Liberia, a community that had welcomed me with open arms and offered its numerous riches.

Monteverde

The foggy morning air in Monteverde seemed like a loving hug, embracing me in a cold, refreshing welcome as I arrived in this wonderful location. Nestled high in the Tilarán Mountains, Monteverde is a spot where the clouds descend to meet the forest, producing a surreal panorama that appears right out of a fairy tale. My trek to Monteverde was a sequence of awe-inspiring experiences, each one enhancing my love for this special part of Costa Rica.

My first excursion led me to the Monteverde Cloud Forest Reserve, a site famous for its biodiversity and ethereal beauty. As I went onto the paths, the forest wrapped me in a green canopy, with moss-covered trees and exquisite orchids covering every limb. The air was rich with the aroma of moist soil and the sounds of nature, from the distant cry of a quetzal to the flutter of leaves underfoot.

Walking over the suspension bridges, I felt as if I was flying through the skies, with the forest extending out under me in all its splendour.

One of the highlights of my vacation was a guided night walk into the cloud forest. As the sun sank and darkness descended, the woodland came alive with nocturnal wildlife. Armed with a flashlight, I followed my guide around the meandering trails, our beams of light unveiling the hidden world of the night. We observed everything from small, brilliant mushrooms to the rare kinkajou, its eyes gleaming in the darkness. The encounter was both exhilarating and sobering, a reminder of the enormous variety of species that survives in this particular habitat.

Monteverde is also home to a flourishing community of artists and craftspeople. In the little town of Santa Elena, I found a plethora of galleries and studios displaying local goods. One specific store grabbed my attention, packed with amazing wood sculptures and bright paintings. The artist, a nice local, told how the natural beauty of Monteverde inspired his work. I couldn't resist buying a wonderfully carved hummingbird, a lovely remembrance of my stay in this amazing area.

The region's devotion to sustainability and conservation is visible wherever you look. I visited a local coffee plantation, where I learnt about the organic agricultural procedures that help maintain the delicate balance of the ecology. The trip was both instructive and tasty, as I tried some of the best coffee I've ever tasted, each sip a monument to the care and passion of the growers.

For those seeking adventure, Monteverde provides a wealth of activities. I couldn't pass up the chance to go zip-lining, and the experience did not disappoint. Soaring over the trees, with the forest racing by in a swirl of green, was an exciting sensation. The views from the platforms were stunning, affording a bird's-eye perspective of the verdant environment below.

Another wonderful experience was visiting the Monteverde Butterfly Garden. Walking through the enclosed gardens, surrounded by flying butterflies of every hue and size, was like walking into a living kaleidoscope. The experienced staff gave intriguing insights about the life cycles and habits of these fragile animals, bringing another depth of amazement to the encounter.

As my stay in Monteverde came to a conclusion, I found myself ruminating on the numerous marvels I had experienced. This location, with its misty trees and thriving population, had caught my heart in a way few places ever do. The memories of my excursions, from the tranquil beauty of the cloud forest to the exhilaration of zip-lining, will linger with me long after I depart.

Monteverde is more than simply a destination; it is a tribute to the beauty and resilience of nature. It is a place where the spirit of conservation and community flourishes, where every corner contains a new discovery, and where the enchantment of the cloud forest leaves an unforgettable impact on those who come. As I boarded the bus to my next destination, I knew that Monteverde had become a part of me, a beloved chapter in my trip across Costa Rica.

La Fortuna

The first rays of dawn illuminated the sky in shades of pink and gold as I arrived in La Fortuna, a charming hamlet perched at the foot of the magnificent Arenal Volcano. The air was crisp and filled with the promise of adventure, and I felt a rush of excitement as I went out to explore this lovely place. La Fortuna, with its beautiful surroundings and active town, is a gem in Costa Rica's crown, presenting a perfect combination of natural beauty and cultural depth.

My adventure started with a visit to the Arenal Volcano National Park, a must-see for every tourist visiting La Fortuna. The park's paths meander through deep rainforests, past old lava fields, and give stunning views of the volcano itself. As I climbed, the noises of the jungle surrounded me — the cries of exotic birds, the rustling of leaves, and the distant scream of howler monkeys. Reaching a viewpoint, I gazed in awe of the volcano's enormous grandeur, its top sometimes veiled in mist, adding to its mystery.

One of the most unforgettable experiences at La Fortuna was seeing the La Fortuna Waterfall. Tucked secluded in a beautiful forest, the waterfall rushed down a high cliff into a crystal-clear pool below. The climb to the falls was exhilarating, and the sight of the water tumbling into the green pool was nothing short of stunning. I couldn't resist having a relaxing bath in the chilly waters, surrounded by the tranquil beauty of the jungle.

La Fortuna is also noted for its hot springs, a natural result of the geothermal activity from the Arenal Volcano. I spent a delightful day at one of the several hot spring resorts, basking in the warm, mineral-rich waters. The experience was wonderfully calming, and the lovely tropical vegetation around the pools contributed to the feeling of serenity. It was the ideal way to relax after a day of adventure.

The town of La Fortuna itself is attractive and bustling, with a friendly environment that quickly makes you feel at home. The central park, with its wonderfully designed gardens and the historic Parroquia San Juan Bosco church, is the centre of the town. I liked leisurely strolls in the park, frequently stopping to speak with residents and other tourists. The town's streets are dotted with a variety of stores, cafés, and restaurants, each giving a flavour of local culture and food.

One of the highlights of my stay was a tour of a local chocolate farm. The trip gave a fascinating insight into the process of cultivating, harvesting, and manufacturing chocolate. I learnt about the history of cacao in Costa Rica and got the chance to try some of the greatest chocolate I've ever eaten. The rich, nuanced tastes were a monument to the passion and competence of the local farmers.

For those seeking adventure, La Fortuna provides a wealth of activities. I couldn't resist the exhilaration of zip-lining through the jungle canopy. The adrenaline rush of flying above the trees, with the gorgeous panorama spreading below, was a memorable experience. Another thrilling activity was white-water rafting on the Balsa River. The rapids gave exactly the perfect blend of thrill and difficulty, and the surrounding landscape was just spectacular.

As my stay in La Fortuna came to an end, I pondered on the various marvels I had experienced. This location, with its stunning scenery and dynamic people, had given a wonderful combination of action and leisure. The recollections of my experiences, from the awe-inspiring vistas of Arenal Volcano to the tranquil serenity of the hot springs, will linger with me long after I departed.

La Fortuna is more than simply a vacation; it is a monument to the natural beauty and cultural diversity of Costa Rica. It is a location where the spirit of adventure and the friendliness of the local people come together to produce an amazing experience. As I boarded the bus to my next destination, I knew that La Fortuna had left an everlasting stamp on my heart, a beloved chapter in my trip across this magnificent country.

Manuel Antonio

The early morning mist clung to the thick vegetation as I made my way to Manuel Antonio, a seaside treasure that promised a combination of natural magnificence and dynamic culture. Nestled between the busy town of Quepos and the calm expanse of Manuel Antonio National Park, this location is a microcosm of Costa Rica's exceptional beauty and biodiversity. My voyage to Manuel Antonio was a sequence of remarkable events, each one more enthralling than the previous.

My first trip was to Manuel Antonio National Park, a refuge that offers some of the most beautiful beaches and varied fauna in the country. As I approached the park, the symphony of nature surrounded me — the sounds of howler monkeys, the rustling of leaves, and the distant crash of waves. The park's pathways took me through deep rainforests, where I met white-faced capuchin monkeys gleefully swinging from trees and bright toucans sitting high in the canopy. The sight of a sloth casually swinging from a branch was a delight, a reminder of the park's tremendous biodiversity.

The beaches inside the park were nothing short of magnificent. Playa Manuel Antonio, with its pristine white sand and turquoise waves, was a fantastic site for leisure. I spent hours swimming in the warm, clear waters and resting beneath the shade of palm palms. The isolated coves and secret beaches created a feeling of peace that was hard to obtain anywhere. Each beach has its own particular appeal, from the crowded Playa Espadilla to the more quiet Playa Gemelas.

Beyond the natural beauty, Manuel Antonio is a hotspot of adventure and excitement. I couldn't resist the exhilaration of zip-lining through the jungle canopy. The adrenaline rush of flying above the trees, with the gorgeous panorama spreading below, was an experience I will never forget. The guides were informed and ensured a safe and exciting journey, sharing insights into the ecology and animals of the area as we zoomed from platform to platform.

Kayaking in the mangroves was another wonderful experience. Paddling across the tranquil streams, I felt a great connection to the natural environment. The mangroves, with their complicated root systems and numerous fauna, were a refuge of serenity. I noticed a variety of species, including herons and kingfishers, and even got a glimpse of a crocodile lounging on the riverside. The tranquillity of the mangroves contrasted well with the lively bustle of the metropolis.

The town of Manuel Antonio itself is a wonderful combination of local culture and contemporary comforts. The main thoroughfare, dotted with a variety of stores, cafés, and restaurants, gave a flavour of local life. I liked leisurely strolls across the town, enjoying great Costa Rican food and perusing the colourful marketplaces. The local craftsmen presented their goods, from handcrafted jewellery to bright paintings, each item representing the essence of the area.

One of the most memorable nights was spent eating at a cliffside restaurant, where I had a magnificent dinner while watching the sun set over the Pacific Ocean. The sky changed into a palette of oranges, pinks, and purples, giving a magnificent light over the area. The sound of the waves crashing against the rocks below added to the mood, making a beautiful finale to a day of exploring.

As my stay in Manuel Antonio drew to a conclusion, I pondered on the various marvels I had encountered. This area, with its amazing natural beauty and lively culture, had left an unforgettable impact on my heart. The memories of my travels, from the tranquil beaches to the exhilarating zip-line, will linger with me long after I depart.

Manuel Antonio is more than simply a destination; it is a monument to the beauty and variety of Costa Rica. It is a location where the spirit of adventure and the friendliness of the local people come together to produce an amazing experience. As I boarded the bus to my next destination, I knew that Manuel Antonio had become a beloved chapter in my trip through this magnificent country.

Tamarindo

The salty breath of the Pacific Ocean met me when I arrived in Tamarindo, a bustling seaside town that pulses with the beat of the waves. Known for its magnificent beaches and vibrant environment, Tamarindo is a refuge for surfers, sun-seekers, and explorers alike. Nestled in the Guanacaste region, this town provides a great combination of natural beauty and contemporary conveniences, making it an excellent location for anybody wishing to enjoy the finest of Costa Rica.

My first morning at Tamarindo was spent visiting its famed beach, a vast expanse of golden sand lapped by the blue seas of the Pacific. The beach is a mecca for surfers, with waves that appeal to both novices and seasoned experts. I decided to take a surfing class, and under the direction of a local instructor, I managed to catch my first wave. The pleasure of riding the wave was unrivalled, and I immediately realised why Tamarindo is regarded as one of Costa Rica's finest surf locations.

Beyond the waves, Tamarindo's beaches offer a wealth of activities. I spent hours snorkelling in the beautiful seas, uncovering a rich underwater world alive with colourful fish and coral. Kayaking down the coast presented a distinct view of the seashore, with its hidden bays and rocky outcrops. Each day finished with a spectacular sunset, the sky blazing with shades of orange and pink, creating a lovely light over the water.

The town of Tamarindo itself is a buzzing centre of activity. The main street is dotted with an assortment of stores, cafés, and restaurants, each giving a flavour of local culture and food. I liked leisurely strolls around the town, trying excellent Costa Rican foods like ceviche and casado, and perusing the artisan shops for unusual gifts. The active nightlife of Tamarindo is another highlight, with seaside bars and clubs providing live music and dancing well into the night.

One of the most unforgettable experiences in Tamarindo was visiting the adjacent Marino Las Baulas National Park. This protected area is an important breeding location for the endangered leatherback turtles. I took a guided night tour, and under the cover of darkness, we observed these wonderful animals make their way up the beach to deposit their eggs. It was a sobering and awe-inspiring sight, a reminder of the fragile balance of nature and the need for conservation efforts.

For those seeking excitement, Tamarindo offers a selection of fascinating activities. I proceeded on an ATV journey into the surrounding area, traversing rocky routes and enjoying panoramic views of the coastline. Horseback riding down the beach at dusk was another wonderful experience, the rhythmic sound of hooves on sand creating a tranquil and timeless moment.

The adjacent town of Santa Cruz, considered as the legendary capital of Costa Rica, provides a greater glimpse into the region's cultural legacy. I went during one of their annual festivals, when the streets were alive with music, dancing, and beautiful costumes. The enthusiasm and passion of the local people were intoxicating, and I found myself caught up in the festivities, dancing and laughing with new friends.

As my stay in Tamarindo drew to a conclusion, I pondered on the various events that had made my vacation so unique. From the excitement of surfing to the peacefulness of a sunset horseback ride, Tamarindo had given a perfect combination of action and leisure. The memories of my time here, from the busy town to the breathtaking natural settings, will remain with me long after I depart.

Tamarindo is more than simply a beach town; it is a lively community that represents the essence of Costa Rica. It is a location where the beauty of nature and the kindness of the local people come together to produce an amazing experience. As I boarded the bus to my next destination, I knew that Tamarindo had left an everlasting stamp on my heart, a beloved chapter in my trip through this magnificent country.

Puerto Viejo

The rhythmic sound of reggae music filled the air as I got off the bus at Puerto Viejo, a thriving town on Costa Rica's Caribbean coast. Known for its laid-back environment and spectacular natural beauty, Puerto Viejo is a location where the speed of life slows down, encouraging you to rest and immerse yourself in its distinct culture. This town, with its Afro-Caribbean origins, provides a distinct taste of Costa Rica, one that is rich in history, culture, and natural beauties.

My first day in Puerto Viejo was spent visiting the town itself. The bright buildings, covered with murals and street art, represented the exuberant energy of the neighbourhood. The main street was lined with an eclectic mix of stores, cafés, and restaurants, each giving a sense of local life. I went through the marketplaces, where sellers offered everything from homemade trinkets to fresh tropical fruits. The perfume of Caribbean spices filled the air, and I couldn't resist eating some of the traditional specialties, such rice and beans cooked in coconut milk and spicy jerk chicken.

One of the pleasures of my stay was a bike ride down the shore. Renting a bicycle was uncomplicated, and it enabled me to explore the region at my own leisure. The coastal route afforded spectacular views of the ocean, with its turquoise waves and picturesque beaches. I made numerous stops along the road, each one exposing a new dimension of Puerto Viejo's natural beauty. Playa Cocles, with its golden beaches and beautiful surf, was a favoured place for both residents and visitors. I spent a peaceful day here, swimming in the warm waves and soaking up the sun.

A short trip from the town led me to the Gandoca-Manzanillo National animal Refuge, a paradise for animal aficionados. The refuge is home to a vast assortment of flora and animals, from howler monkeys and sloths to colourful toucans and parrots. I attended a guided tour, which gave intriguing insights into the environment and the attempts to conserve it. Walking through the lush jungle, I felt a great connection to nature, enveloped by the sights and sounds of the rainforest.

Puerto Viejo is also a gateway to some of the top snorkelling and diving destinations in Costa Rica. I took a boat excursion to the adjacent coral reefs, where I was delighted with a lively underwater environment. The pure waters provided for good vision, and I marvelled at the brilliant coral formations and the plethora of fish that swam about me. It was a remarkable event, one that emphasised the great biodiversity of the area.

The town's nightlife is another characteristic that makes Puerto Viejo unique. As the sun dropped, the town came alive with music and dancing. I found myself pulled to a seaside bar, where the sounds of reggae and calypso filled the night air. The mood was fantastic, with residents and tourists alike dancing beneath the stars. It was a beautiful finale to a day of discovery, a celebration of the diverse culture that distinguishes Puerto Viejo.

One of the most unforgettable experiences was visiting the Jaguar Rescue Center, a refuge devoted to the rehabilitation and release of wounded and orphaned animals. The centre's workers were enthusiastic and informed, and their devotion to animal protection was incredibly motivating. I got the chance to witness a range of creatures up close, from lively monkeys to magnificent birds of prey.

The excursion was both instructive and comforting, a monument to the significance of maintaining Costa Rica's natural legacy.

As my stay in Puerto Viejo drew to a conclusion, I pondered on the various events that had made my vacation so remarkable. From the bustling town and its friendly inhabitants to the breathtaking natural settings and rich cultural legacy, Puerto Viejo had delivered a unique and remarkable peek into the heart of Costa Rica. The memories of my exploits, from diving in the coral reefs to dancing beneath the moonlight, will linger with me long after I depart.

Puerto Viejo is more than simply a vacation; it is a celebration of life, culture, and environment. It is a location where the spirit of the Caribbean comes alive, asking you to slow down, relax, and absorb the beauty of the moment. As I boarded the bus to my next destination, I knew that Puerto Viejo had left an everlasting stamp on my heart, a beloved chapter in my trip across this magnificent country.

Nosara

The early morning light shed a golden glow over the calm beaches of Nosara, a hidden treasure on Costa Rica's Nicoya Peninsula. Known for its scenic coastline and laid-back environment, Nosara is a refuge for anyone seeking both adventure and leisure. As I arrived in this delightful village, I had an instant feeling of tranquillity and enthusiasm, anxious to see everything that Nosara has to offer.

My first day in Nosara was spent at Playa Guiones, a gorgeous beach famed for its reliable surf breaks. The beach extended for kilometres, its golden sands meeting the blue seas of the Pacific. I opted to take a surfing class, and under the supervision of a local teacher, I rapidly found myself riding the waves. The exhilaration of surfing in such a magnificent location was unsurpassed, and I understood why Nosara is regarded as a top destination for surfers from across the globe.

Beyond the waves, Nosara's beaches provided a range of activities. I spent hours going down the coastline, gathering seashells and enjoying the quiet beauty of the countryside. The sunsets at Nosara were especially stunning, with the sky changing into a tapestry of vivid hues as the sun fell below the horizon. Each evening, residents and tourists alike came on the beach to witness this daily display, establishing a feeling of community and shared admiration for nature's grandeur.

Nosara is also noted for its devotion to health and sustainability. I visited numerous yoga studios, each providing lessons that suited to all levels of expertise. Practising yoga in an open-air studio, with the sounds of the ocean and the rustling of palm trees in the backdrop, was a truly revitalising experience. The town's focus on holistic living extended to its food as well. I appreciated meals at local restaurants that concentrated on fresh, organic products, with dishes that were both tasty and healthy.

One of the pleasures of my tour was visiting the Nosara Biological Reserve. This protected region is home to a rich assortment of wildlife, from howler monkeys and iguanas to a variety of bird species. I attended a guided tour, which gave intriguing insights into the local environment and the attempts to conserve it. Walking around the reserve, I felt a strong connection to nature, enveloped by the sights and sounds of the rainforest.

Nosara's spirit of community was obvious in its thriving local culture. The town's marketplaces were a veritable trove of handcrafted items, from finely woven fabrics to wonderfully carved wooden sculptures. I spent hours perusing the booths, interacting with the craftspeople, and learning about their trade. The kindness and openness of the local folks made me feel welcome and at home.

For those seeking adventure, Nosara offers a choice of outdoor activities. I engaged on a horseback riding excursion down the shore, an experience that was both exciting and tranquil. Riding down the coastline, with the waves crashing close and the wind in my hair, was a moment of pure ecstasy. Another wonderful event was kayaking in the mangroves, where I observed a vast variety of species and enjoyed the calm of the rivers.

As my stay in Nosara drew to a conclusion, I pondered on the various events that had made my vacation so unique. From the excitement of surfing to the calm of yoga, Nosara has given a wonderful combination of action and leisure. The memories of my time here, from the magnificent beaches to the colourful local culture, will linger with me long after I departed.

Nosara is more than simply a destination; it is a sanctuary where the beauty of nature and the kindness of the local people come together to produce an amazing experience. As I boarded the bus to my next destination, I knew that Nosara had left an everlasting stamp on my heart, a beloved chapter in my trip through this magnificent country.

Dominical

Located on Costa Rica's southern Pacific coast, Dominical is a tiny, laid-back beach town that provides a unique combination of natural beauty, adventure, and calm. Known for its magnificent beaches, lush woods, and dynamic community, Dominical is a location that captivates the hearts of everyone who comes.

Dominical's beaches are a surfer's dream, with regular waves that draw aficionados from across the globe. The major beach, Playa Dominical, is famed for its fierce surf and breathtaking sunsets. For those wanting a more leisurely experience, adjacent Playa Dominicalito provides calmer seas and a gorgeous environment great for swimming and sunbathing.

For adventure lovers, Dominical offers a gateway to some of Costa Rica's most spectacular activities. The Nauyaca Waterfalls, only a short drive from town, are a must-visit. These impressive falls, with a total drop of almost 200 feet, provide a refreshing natural pool for swimming and a beautiful setting for pictures. Whether you want to trek, ride horseback, or take a truck tour, the route to the falls is an experience in itself.

Dominical is surrounded by lush forests and different ecosystems, giving it a sanctuary for wildlife enthusiasts. The Hacienda Barú animal Refuge is a renowned place for birding and animal trips. With over 330 species of birds and a variety of animals, including monkeys and sloths, the refuge gives a look into Costa Rica's vast biodiversity. Guided excursions give deeper insights into the flora and animals, enriching the experience.

The town of Dominical boasts a laid-back, bohemian feel, drawing a mix of surfers, digital nomads, and long-time expats. The main street is dotted with unique stores, cafés, and restaurants, each giving a sense of local culture. The weekly farmers' market is a highlight, where you may discover fresh fruit, homemade crafts, and delectable local delights. The community's devotion to sustainability and organic living is obvious in the profusion of natural food outlets and eco-friendly companies.

For those seeking relaxation, Dominical provides a range of wellness activities. Yoga studios and health resorts are sprinkled across the area, offering tranquil settings for meditation and recuperation. The peaceful beaches and lush surroundings offer the ideal atmosphere for relaxing and reconnecting with nature.

Dominical is more than simply a beach town; it is a lively community that represents the essence of Costa Rica. With its breathtaking natural surroundings, exhilarating activities, and inviting attitude, Dominical provides an exceptional experience for every tourist. Whether you're surfing the waves, exploring the rainforests, or just soaking up the sun, Dominical is a place that will leave you with lasting memories and a profound appreciation for the beauty of Costa Rica.

Chapter Nine: EXPERIENCE

Staying Safe in Costa Rica

Costa Rica is a lovely and hospitable country, but like any tourist location, it's crucial to keep conscious of your safety. Here are some extensive guidelines to help you have a safe and happy trip:

General Safety Tips

1. Stay Aware of Your Surroundings
Always be alert of your surroundings, particularly in congested settings like markets and bus stops. Petty theft, such as pickpocketing, might occur, so keep your stuff safe and avoid flaunting valuables like costly jewellery or devices.

2. Travel During the Day
While Costa Rica is typically secure, it's advisable to go during daytime hours. If you must go at night, stay in well-lit and busy places. Avoid wandering alone after dark, especially in unfamiliar regions.

3. Use Reputable Transportation
Opt for official taxis (red with a yellow triangle) or ride-sharing services. If you're renting a vehicle, ensure it's from a respected firm and always lock your doors. Be wary of leaving valuables in your vehicle, particularly in plain sight.

4. Secure Your Accommodations
Choose lodgings with decent evaluations and security precautions. Many hotels and hostels provide safes for keeping valuables. Always lock your doors and windows, even while you're inside.

Health and Wellness

1. Stay Hydrated and Use Sunscreen
Costa Rica's tropical climate may be severe. Drink lots of water and wear sunscreen to protect yourself from the sun's rays. Wearing a hat and sunglasses might also assist.

2. Be Mindful of Food and Water
Stick to bottled or filtered water, particularly in remote locations. Enjoy the local cuisine, but ensure that food is prepared well and served hot. Be careful with street food and go for crowded vendors where the turnover is high.

3. Protect Against Mosquitoes

Mosquitoes may bring illnesses like dengue and Zika. Use insect repellent, wear long sleeves and trousers in the evening, and sleep beneath a mosquito net if required. Many rooms include nets or have protected windows.

Adventure Activities

1. Choose Licensed Tour Operators

Costa Rica is recognized for its adventure sports, from zip-lining to white-water rafting. Always pick legal and trustworthy tour providers. Check reviews and ensure they follow safety guidelines.

2. Follow Safety Instructions

Whether you're hiking, surfing, or touring a national park, always observe the safety precautions offered by guides and signage. Stay on defined paths and be mindful of your limitations.

3. Respect Wildlife

Costa Rica's wildlife is magnificent, but it's necessary to see creatures from a distance. Do not feed or try to touch them. Use a zoom lens for images and observe rules for animal interactions.

Emergency Preparedness

1. Keep Emergency Numbers Handy
Familiarise oneself with local emergency numbers. The universal emergency number in Costa Rica is 911. It's also helpful to have the contact information for your country's embassy or consulate.

2. Have Travel Insurance
Travel insurance may give peace of mind in case of medical crises, trip cancellations, or misplaced possessions. Ensure your insurance covers the activities you want to conduct.

3. Share Your Itinerary
Let someone at home know your trip intentions and check in periodically. This might be beneficial in case of an emergency.

Cultural Considerations

1. Respect Local Customs
Costa Ricans, or Ticos, are recognized for their warmth and kindness. Show respect for local customs and traditions. Learning a few simple words in Spanish may go a long way in creating rapport.

2. Be Environmentally Conscious
Costa Rica is a leader in ecotourism. Respect the environment by avoiding littering, keeping on authorised trails, and supporting sustainable activities. Many locations have strong rules to safeguard the natural beauty and animals.

Staying safe in Costa Rica is primarily about being attentive and prepared. By following these suggestions, you may enjoy all the great activities this lovely nation has to offer while ensuring your vacation is safe and enjoyable. Whether you're touring the colourful towns, resting on the gorgeous beaches, or hiking through the lush jungles, a little prudence and common sense can go a long way in making your Costa Rican journey memorable.

Wildlife Watching (e.g., Sloths, Monkeys, Turtles)

Costa Rica is a heaven for wildlife aficionados, presenting a complex tapestry of habitats that are home to an astounding variety of creatures. Whether you're visiting lush rainforests, gorgeous beaches, or calm mangroves, you're likely to meet some of the country's most recognizable wildlife.

Here's a guide to some of the greatest spots and advice for wildlife viewing in Costa Rica.

Sloths

Sloths are among the most adored creatures in Costa Rica, recognized for their sluggish movements and adorable expressions. You may locate both two-toed and three-toed sloths in different sections of the nation.

- **Manuel Antonio National Park:** This park is an excellent site to view sloths relaxing in the trees. The park's well-maintained paths make it accessible for all ages.
- **Cahuita National Park:** Located on the Caribbean coast, this park provides good possibilities to witness sloths in their native environment.
- **Monteverde Cloud Forest Reserve:** The thick canopy of Monteverde is another great place for sloth sightings, particularly during guided night excursions.

Monkeys

Costa Rica is home to four kinds of monkeys: the howler monkey, spider monkey, white-faced capuchin, and squirrel monkey.

- **-Corcovado National Park:** This park on the Osa Peninsula is one of the greatest sites to observe all four types of monkeys. The park's distant location and diversified ecosystems make it a sanctuary for animals.
- **-Tortuguero National Park:** Known for its network of canals and abundant wildlife, Tortuguero is a fantastic site for seeing howler and spider monkeys.
- **-Santa Rosa National Park:** Located in the Guanacaste area, this park is a fantastic site to watch white-faced capuchins and howler monkeys.

Turtles

Costa Rica's beaches are critical breeding grounds for

various species of sea turtles, including the leatherback, green, hawksbill, and olive ridley turtles.

- **-Tortuguero National Park:** This park is notable for its turtle breeding places. The optimum time to visit is during the nesting season, which runs from July to October for green turtles and February to April for leatherbacks.
- **Ostional Wildlife Refuge:** Located on the Nicoya Peninsula, Ostional is one of the few spots in the world where you can watch the mass nesting event of olive ridley turtles, known as a "arribada."
- **-Gandoca-Manzanillo Wildlife Refuge:** This refuge on the Caribbean coast is another major nesting place for leatherback turtles.

Birds

Costa Rica is a birdwatcher's delight, with over 900 species documented.

- **-Monteverde Cloud Forest Reserve:** Known for its great biodiversity, Monteverde is a hotspot for birding, including sightings of the resplendent quetzal.

- **-Carara National Park:** Located on the Pacific coast, this park is home to a variety of bird species, including scarlet macaws.
- **-Caño Negro Wildlife Refuge:** This wetland region in northern Costa Rica is a home for ducks and migratory birds.

Tips for Wildlife Watching

- **Hire a Guide:** Local guides are educated about the best sites and times to encounter animals. They can also assist you identify creatures that you would miss on your own.
- **Be Patient and Quiet:** Wildlife viewing demands patience. Move gently and softly to avoid disturbing the animals.
- **Use Binoculars:** A decent set of binoculars may improve your wildlife watching experience, enabling you to observe creatures up close without disturbing them.
- **Respect Wildlife:** Always view animals from a distance. Do not feed or try to touch them, since this may be detrimental to both you and the animals.

Costa Rica's dedication to conservation and its unique ecosystems make it one of the top sites in the world for wildlife viewing. Whether you're looking to witness sloths hanging from the trees, monkeys swinging through the canopy, or turtles breeding on the beaches, Costa Rica provides memorable encounters for nature enthusiasts. So grab your binoculars, hire a skilled guide, and get ready to discover the magnificent wildlife of this wonderful nation.

Canopy Tours and Ziplining

Costa Rica is famous for its lush rainforests and gorgeous vistas, making it an excellent location for canopy tours and ziplining excursions. These activities provide a unique opportunity to enjoy the country's natural beauty from above, giving both adrenaline-pumping exhilaration and magnificent vistas. Here's an in-depth look at some of the greatest spots and suggestions for enjoying canopy tours and ziplining in Costa Rica.

Top Canopy Tours and Ziplining Destinations

Monteverde

Monteverde is one of the most recognized sites for canopy tours in Costa Rica. The cloud forest here offers a fantastic background for ziplining excursions.

- **100% Aventura:** Known for its extreme zipline, this trip includes a Tarzan swing and a superman zipline, delivering a thrilling experience high above the forest canopy. I recall the surge of excitement when I made my first jump off the platform, feeling like I was soaring over the heavens.
- **Sky Adventures:** This trip combines ziplining with hanging bridges and an aerial tram, offering a thorough view of the cloud forest from numerous positions. The aerial tram ride was a peaceful precursor to the heart-pounding ziplines, allowing a chance to drink in the splendour of Monteverde from above.

Arenal

The Arenal area, with its famed volcano, is another great site for ziplining.

- **Arenal Reserve:** This excursion involves an aerial tram ride up the mountain, followed by a series of exciting ziplines that fall through the jungle. The view of Arenal

Volcano from the zipline was incredibly stunning, a sight I'll never forget.

- **Ecoglide Arenal Park:** Known for its safety and family-friendly setting, this park provides a range of zipline alternatives, including a Tarzan swing for additional fun. Swinging through the branches like Tarzan was a boyhood fantasy come true!

Manuel Antonio

Manuel Antonio is not only notable for its national park but also for its canopy excursions.

- **Canopy Safari:** This excursion provides a combination of ziplining, rappelling, and a Tarzan swing, all located in the gorgeous jungle near Manuel Antonio. The mix of activities provided for an action-packed day, and the guides were wonderful at making everyone feel comfortable and thrilled.
- **El Santuario Canopy Adventure:** Featuring some of the longest ziplines in Central America, this trip affords stunning views of the Pacific shoreline and the surrounding forest. The sense of flying above the trees with the ocean in the background was just amazing.

Guanacaste

The arid woods of Guanacaste provide a distinct but equally spectacular zip lining experience.

- **-Diamante Eco Adventure Park:** Home to the famed Superman zipline, this park provides a unique view as you fly face-first over the trees and shoreline. The Superman zipline was an amazing experience, giving me the impression of soaring like a superhero.
- **Witch's Rock Canopy trip:** Located near the shore, this trip combines ziplining with spectacular ocean views and the opportunity to meet local animals. The combination of woodland and seaside vistas made this excursion extra spectacular.

Tips for a Safe and Enjoyable Experience

1. Choose Reputable Operators

Always arrange your canopy tours and ziplining experiences with trustworthy operators that stress safety. Look for firms with strong ratings and qualifications.

2. Wear Appropriate Clothing
Dress comfortably with lightweight, breathable clothes. Closed-toe shoes are a requirement, and long pants may assist protect your legs from any bushes or insects.

3. Follow Safety Instructions
Listen closely to the safety briefing delivered by your guides. Ensure your harness is fastened appropriately and follow all directions throughout the trip.

4. Stay Hydrated
Costa Rica's temperature may be hot and humid, so be sure to drink enough water before and throughout your vacation.

5. Bring a Camera
Many trips provide the opportunity to hire a GoPro or have professional images shot. If you bring your own camera, ensure it's securely attached to prevent losing it mid-zipline.

Canopy excursions and ziplining in Costa Rica provide an unrivalled chance to see the country's natural beauty and wildlife. Whether you're flying over the cloud forests of Monteverde, gliding past the Arenal Volcano, or enjoying the coastline vistas in Guanacaste, these excursions produce unique memories. By picking reliable operators and following safety standards, you can assure an exciting and safe trip that shows the finest of Costa Rica's gorgeous surroundings. My personal experiences on these excursions have left me with a great appreciation for the beauty and excitement that Costa Rica has to offer.

Rafting And Kayaking Adventures

The excitement of adventure was evident as I prepared for my first white-water rafting excursion in Costa Rica. Known for its various and demanding rivers, Costa Rica provides some of the greatest rafting and kayaking activities in the world. From the minute I plunged my paddle into the surging waves, I knew I was in for an incredible experience.

Rafting Adventures

Pacuare River

My experience started on the Pacuare River, generally considered as one of the finest white-water rafting sites internationally. The river runs through lush jungles and steep gorges, giving a combination of exciting rapids and tranquil sections. As we manoeuvred the Class III and IV rapids, the adrenaline rush was fantastic. The guides were skilled and guaranteed our safety while making the excursion fun and educational. Between the rapids, we had opportunities to absorb the spectacular surroundings, observing toucans and even a sloth hanging from a tree.

Sarapiquí River

Next, I travelled to the Sarapiquí River, noted for its accessibility and diversity of rapids ideal for all ability levels. The river's Class II and III rapids offered a wonderful blend of excitement and ease, making it excellent for both novices and seasoned rafters. The verdant surroundings and the odd sighting of monkeys and iguanas added to the thrill. The highlight was a peaceful portion when we could jump into the water and float beside the raft, experiencing the cold river against the scorching heat.

Kayaking Adventures

Tortuguero National Park

For a quieter experience, I travelled to Tortuguero National Park, where kayaking through the complicated network of canals and lagoons gave a new type of excitement. Paddling softly across the river, I felt a strong connection to nature. The park is a sanctuary for wildlife, and I was fortunate enough to observe caimans sunning on the banks, herons fishing in the shallows, and even a manatee flowing smoothly under my kayak. The serenity of the mangroves and the vast variety made this an amazing experience.

Golfo Dulce

Another kayaking pleasure was exploring the Golfo Dulce, a gorgeous gulf on the southern Pacific coast. The quiet, clear waters were great for kayaking, and the neighbouring rainforest offered a lovely background. As I paddled around the shore, I saw playful dolphins and observed marine turtles swimming close. The gulf is also famed for its bioluminescent waters, and a night kayaking excursion showed the amazing light of the sea with each stroke of my paddle.

Tips for a Safe and Enjoyable Adventure

1. Choose Reputable Operators
Always arrange your rafting and kayaking trips with trustworthy operators that value safety. Look for firms with high ratings and competent guides.

2. Wear Appropriate Gear
Dress comfortably in quick-drying garments and wear water shoes or sandals with excellent traction. A helmet and life jacket are needed for rafting, and many operators offer both.

3. Follow Safety Instructions
Listen closely to the safety briefing delivered by your guides. Ensure your gear is suited appropriately and follow all directions throughout the journey.

4. Stay Hydrated

Costa Rica's temperature may be hot and humid, so be sure to drink enough water before and throughout your vacation.

5. Bring a Waterproof Camera
Capture the gorgeous environment and your exhilarating moments on the water. Ensure your camera is properly attached to prevent losing it in the river.

Rafting and kayaking in Costa Rica provide an unrivalled chance to see the country's natural beauty and wildlife. Whether you're negotiating the exhilarating rapids of the Pacuare River or kayaking through the peaceful canals of Tortuguero, these activities produce unique memories. My personal experiences on these excursions have left me with a great appreciation for the beauty and excitement that Costa Rica has to offer. So take your paddle, enjoy the adventure, and get ready to explore the amazing rivers of this lovely nation.

Surfing and Water Sports

The draw of Costa Rica's gorgeous beaches and warm seas is alluring, particularly for those who enjoy surfing and water sports. My tour across this magnificent nation was packed with exhilarating experiences on the waves and quiet moments on the ocean. Here's a glance into some of the top sites and experiences for surfing and water sports in Costa Rica.

Surfing Adventures

Tamarindo

Tamarindo is a thriving beach town on the Pacific coast, noted for its consistent waves and strong surf culture. My first surfing lesson here was memorable. The instructors were attentive and knowledgeable, leading me through the fundamentals before I caught my first wave. The experience of rising up on the board and riding the wave to shore was fantastic. Tamarindo's beach break is suitable for novices, but more experienced surfers may find tough waves farther out.

Santa Teresa

Santa Teresa, with its laid-back feel and magnificent beaches, rapidly became one of my favourite destinations. The waves here are strong and constant, making it a hotspot for surfers from across the globe. I spent my days surfing the waves and my nights watching the sun set over the water, a wonderful combination of excitement and tranquillity.

Pavones

For those wanting a more distant and tough surf experience, Pavones on the southern Pacific coast is a must-visit. Known for having one of the largest left-hand waves in the world, Pavones provides a unique surfing experience. The trek to get there is part of the experience, and the reward is a wave that appears to continue on forever. I recall the excitement of riding that wave, feeling like I was floating eternally down the ocean.

Water Sports

Snorkeling and Diving in Cahuita

Cahuita National Park on the Caribbean coast provides some of the greatest snorkelling and diving in Costa Rica. The coral reefs here are filled with marine life. I spent hours exploring the underwater environment, marvelling at the colourful fish, sea turtles, and vivid corals. The purity of the water and the variety of marine life made this an amazing experience.

Kayaking in Tortuguero

Kayaking along the canals of Tortuguero National Park was a tranquil and engaging way to observe the region's abundant wildlife. Paddling stealthily along the river, I met caimans, monkeys, and a variety of bird species. The calm of the mangroves and the close interactions with animals make this one of my favourite hobbies.

Stand-Up Paddleboarding on Lake Arenal

Stand-up paddleboarding on Lake Arenal, with the gorgeous Arenal Volcano as a background, was a unique and calm experience. The calm waters of the lake were great for paddleboarding, and the sights were just spectacular. It was a terrific opportunity to unwind and take in the natural beauty of the region.

Tips for a Safe and Enjoyable Experience

1. Choose Reputable Operators
Always arrange your surfing and water sports activities with reliable operators that value safety.

Look for firms with high ratings and skilled teachers.

2. Wear Appropriate Gear
For surfing, a rash guard and board shorts are needed. For snorkelling and diving, ensure you have well-fitting masks and fins. Sunscreen is a requirement for any aquatic activities to protect against the intense tropical sun.

3. Follow Safety Instructions
Listen closely to the safety briefing delivered by your guides. Ensure your equipment is fitted appropriately and follow all directions throughout the activity.

4. Stay Hydrated
Costa Rica's temperature may be hot and humid, so be sure to drink lots of water before and throughout your travels.

5. Respect the Environment
Costa Rica is noted for its devotion to conservation. Always follow recommendations to conserve the natural environment, whether you're surfing, snorkelling, or kayaking.

Surfing and water sports in Costa Rica provide an unrivalled chance to see the country's natural beauty and colourful culture. Whether you're catching waves in Tamarindo, snorkelling in Cahuita, or kayaking through Tortuguero's canals, these excursions produce unique memories. My personal experiences on these waterways have left me with a great respect for the beauty and thrill that Costa Rica has to offer. So take your board or paddle, enjoy the adventure, and get ready to explore the amazing seas of this lovely nation.

Hot Springs and Spa Retreats

The instant I walked into the warm, mineral-rich waters of Costa Rica's hot springs, I had an immediate sensation of relaxation and regeneration. Nestled between lush rainforests and volcanic landscapes, these natural treasures provide a wonderful respite from the rush and bustle of daily life. My voyage through Costa Rica's hot springs and spa getaways was a combination of solitude, elegance, and the healing power of nature.

Arenal Hot Springs

My first visit was the Arenal area, home to some of the most renowned hot springs in Costa Rica. The spectacular Arenal Volcano loomed in the backdrop, its presence lending a bit of mysticism to the event. I visited numerous hot springs here, each having a distinct environment and set of facilities.

Tabacón Thermal Resort & Spa was a highlight. The resort's hot springs are supplied by the Tabacón River, which is heated by the geothermal activity of the volcano. As I rested in the numerous pools, surrounded by gorgeous tropical plants, I felt the tension wash away. The natural backdrop, mixed with the calming warmth of the water, made a genuinely beautiful experience. The resort also provided a variety of spa services, from volcanic mud wraps to deep tissue massages, increasing the overall feeling of well-being.

Another highlight in the Arenal region was The Springs Resort and Spa. This magnificent resort had three hot spring pools, each with various temperatures and settings. I really appreciated the isolated pools, where I could relax in seclusion while listening to the sounds of the jungle. The resort's spa services were fantastic, with treatments that blended local products like coffee and chocolate, bringing a distinct Costa Rican touch to the pampering.

Rincón de la Vieja

Next, I travelled to the Rincon de la Vieja area, noted for its volcanic activity and natural hot springs. The Rio Negro Hot Springs were a marvel. Located inside the Rincon de la Vieja National Park, these springs provided a more rustic and natural experience. I trekked across the park's various landscapes, past boiling mud pots and fumaroles, before reaching the hot springs.

The pools, placed along the Rio Negro River, were surrounded by lush forest, giving a calm and undisturbed setting. The mineral-rich waters were wonderfully calming, and I felt a strong feeling of connection to nature as I rested in the warm pools.

Orosi Valley

The Orosi Valley, with its beautiful scenery and coffee plantations, was another site on my hot springs adventure. The Hacienda Orosi provides a beautiful and personal hot springs experience. The pools, filled with naturally heated mineral water, were placed against a background of undulating hills and beautiful woodlands. The hacienda's spa services centred on relaxation and regeneration, including choices like aromatherapy and hydrotherapy. I spent a delightful day here, alternating between the hot springs and the spa, feeling thoroughly rejuvenated by the conclusion of my stay.

Wellness Retreats

In addition to hot springs, Costa Rica is home to various wellness facilities that provide a comprehensive approach to relaxation and health. The Retreat Costa Rica in the Central Valley was a highlight. This health facility, set on a hilltop with spectacular views of the surrounding countryside, provided a choice of programs centred on physical, emotional, and spiritual well-being. I participated in yoga and meditation classes, savoured organic farm-to-table meals, and indulged in spa treatments that employed natural, locally produced products. The retreat's calm setting and full wellness facilities made it a wonderful location to relax and recover.

My trek across Costa Rica's hot springs and spa getaways was a tribute to the country's natural beauty and devotion to wellbeing. Each place provided a distinct combination of leisure, elegance, and the healing power of nature. Whether bathing in the mineral-rich waters of Arenal, exploring the volcanic scenery of Rincon de la Vieja, or indulging in holistic therapies at a health resort,

I discovered a profound feeling of serenity and refreshment. Costa Rica's hot springs and spa resorts are more than simply places to rest; they are sanctuaries that nurture the body, mind, and spirit.

Local Cooking Classes and Food Tours

The perfume of fresh herbs and spices filled the air as I came into the kitchen for my first Costa Rican cooking session.

Immersing oneself in the local culinary traditions was a great way to absorb the culture and cuisine of this beautiful nation. From busy markets to cosy home kitchens, Costa Rica offers a choice of cooking lessons and cuisine excursions that appeal to all tastes and interests.

Cooking Classes

- **La Fortuna**

In the shadow of the Arenal Volcano, La Fortuna is a terrific site to start your gastronomic trip. I took a cooking class organised by a local family, where I learnt to create traditional Costa Rican cuisine. The adventure started with a visit to the local market, where we picked fresh ingredients including plantains, yucca, and a range of tropical fruits. Back in the kitchen, we produced a lovely lunch of gallo pinto, arroz con pollo, and patacones. The hands-on experience, along with the kindness and generosity of my hosts, made this session extremely unforgettable.

- **Manuel Antonio**

In Manuel Antonio, I participated in a culinary workshop that focused on farm-to-table food. We began the day by visiting a neighbouring organic farm, where we chose fresh veggies and herbs. The training was conducted in an open-air kitchen with beautiful views of the Pacific Ocean. Under the instruction of a talented chef, we cooked a range of delicacies, including ceviche and casado. The highlight was learning to cook tortillas from scratch, a skill I was excited to bring back home.

Food Tours

- **San José**

San José, the capital city, provides a bustling cuisine culture that is best experienced on a guided food tour. I boarded a tour that brought us through the busy Central Market, where we enjoyed a range of local delicacies. From fresh tamales to luscious churros, each mouthful was a new experience.

The trip also featured stops at traditional sodas (small local eateries) where we savoured robust delicacies like olla de carne and sopa negra. The expert guide gave intriguing insights into the history and culture behind each dish, making the experience both instructive and tasty.

- **Puerto Viejo**

On the Caribbean coast, Puerto Viejo is famed for its Afro-Caribbean cuisine. I attended a cuisine tour that emphasised the particular delicacies of this area. We visited local cafes and enjoyed foods like rice and beans cooked in coconut milk, jerk chicken, and rondon (a substantial seafood stew).

The trip also included a visit to a chocolate factory, where we learnt about the traditional ways of chocolate manufacture and tasted some wonderful samples. The colourful tastes and rich cultural legacy of Puerto Viejo made this tour a highlight of my vacation.

Tips for a Great Experience

1. Be Open to New Flavors
Costa Rican food is varied and tasty. Be experimental and explore foods you may not be acquainted with. You could find a new favourite!

2. Engage with Locals
The nicest aspect about cooking workshops and culinary excursions is the ability to engage with locals. Ask questions, exchange tales, and immerse yourself in the culture.

3. Take Notes
If you're participating in a cooking class, take notes on the recipes and procedures. This will enable you to duplicate the recipes at home and share a taste of Costa Rica with friends and family.

4. Wear Comfortable Clothing
Cooking workshops and culinary excursions might include a lot of walking and standing. Wear comfortable attire and shoes to help you enjoy the event to the utmost.

Exploring Costa Rica via its cuisine is a trip that involves all the senses. From the colourful marketplaces of San José to the farm-to-table experiences in Manuel Antonio, each cooking lesson and food tour gives a unique peek into the country's rich culinary legacy. My personal travels in Costa Rican kitchens and marketplaces have left me with a better respect for the tastes and customs of this lovely nation. Whether you're a seasoned chef or an inquisitive eater, Costa Rica's cooking lessons and culinary excursions are guaranteed to create amazing experiences and delectable discoveries.

Chapter Ten: SHOPPING

Best Markets and Shops for Local Goods

When I arrived in Costa Rica for the first time, I was anxious to immerse myself in the culture of the country, and I thought that the best way to accomplish so would be to explore the country's bustling markets and one-of-a-kind stores. The act of shopping in Costa Rica is an experience in and of itself, as it provides a treasure trove of local things that reflect the narrative of this beautiful nation. This is a tour of some of the most exceptional marketplaces and businesses that I came across, each of which had its own unique allure and specialised offerings.

Shopping in San José is like a heartbeat for the local community.

In San José, the busy city, I started my journey through the world of shopping. My first destination was the Central Market, also known as the Mercado Central. In the most positive manner conceivable, this market is an excess of sensory information. While I was making my way down the winding alleyways, I was met by the scent of freshly brewed coffee, the vivid colours of tropical fruits, and the active conversation of the merchants. From handmade leather products to traditional Costa Rican snacks, I was able to get all I needed at this location. One of my most treasured acquisitions was a well woven hammock that was ideal for lounging about in the afternoon.

Just a short walk from the Central Market is the National Craft Market. This shop is a sanctuary for everyone wishing to take home a bit of Costa Rican creativity. The market is crowded with vendors offering handcrafted jewellery, pottery, and wooden sculptures. I spent hours perusing through the complex artwork and conversing with the craftspeople about their trade. Each item had a story, and I couldn't resist purchasing a few keepsakes to remind me of my trip.

Manuel Antonio: A Blend of Nature and Craft

Next, I travelled to Manuel Antonio, a coastal town noted for its lovely national park and beautiful beaches. The village markets here are smaller but no less attractive. The Villa Vanilla Spice Tour & Shop was a lovely surprise. Nestled in the beautiful jungle, this boutique provides a range of organic spices, vanilla extracts, and handcrafted chocolates. I had a tour of the spice farm and learnt about the ecological measures they utilise. The highlight was tasting the freshly produced vanilla ice cream, which was just exquisite.

In the town proper, I came onto Beso Loco Boutique de Playa, a quirky small business offering beachwear and local crafts. The owner's effervescent demeanour and the bright environment make shopping here a delight. I picked up a bright sarong and some handcrafted jewellery, excellent keepsakes of my stay by the water.

Tamarindo: Surf, Sun, and Shopping

Tamarindo, a vibrant beach town on the Pacific coast, was my next visit. The Tama Market, held every Saturday, is a must-visit. This multicultural marketplace is a hotbed of creativity, with sellers offering everything from organic fruit to homemade soaps and jewellery. I appreciated the laid-back attitude and the opportunity to interact with local craftsmen about their work. One of my favourite purchases was a hand-painted porcelain bowl, which now stands proudly on my kitchen table.

The Tamarindo Night Market, conducted on Thursdays, is another attraction. The market comes alive with music, food vendors, and a variety of crafts. I liked trying the local food and picking up interesting gifts like hand-carved wooden sculptures and bright paintings. The enthusiasm of the night market is contagious, making it a fantastic way to conclude a day in Tamarindo.

Jacó: A Shopper's Paradise

Jacó, a famous coastal town, provides a mix of traditional markets and contemporary stores. The Tico Pod Art House & Gifts is a highlight, presenting a broad assortment of handmade products from local artisans. From complex masks to vibrant paintings, the boutique is a testimony to Costa Rica's rich creative tradition. I spent a large portion of the day here, appreciating the artistry and choosing out a few things to take home.

For a more traditional shopping experience, the Jacó Market is the place to go. This market is a veritable trove of local items, from fresh fruit to homemade crafts. I liked perusing the kiosks and conversing with the pleasant sellers. One of my finest buys was a wonderfully made wooden dish, ideal for presenting fresh fruit.

La Fortuna: Souvenirs from the Shadow of Arenal

La Fortuna, noted for its closeness to Arenal Volcano, provides some unique shopping experiences. The town's marketplaces are loaded with locally manufactured items, from coffee to crafts. One of my favourite sites was the Souvenir Leo, a family-run business selling a broad choice of handcrafted products. The proprietors were really warm, and I departed with a bag full of goods, including some great Costa Rican coffee and a hand-carved wooden toucan.

Shopping in Costa Rica is more than simply a shopping experience; it's a trip through the country's culture and customs. Each market and store gives a window into the local way of life, making every purchase a memory to keep. Whether you're seeking unique gifts or simply want to soak up the local vibe, Costa Rica's markets and stores are guaranteed to please.

Local Crafts, Coffee, and Unique Finds (e.g., Handmade Jewelry, Costa Rican Coffee)

When I reflect back on my time in Costa Rica, one of the most memorable memories is the joy of finding local crafts, experiencing the rich scent of freshly brewed coffee, and coming across unexpected items that I never anticipated. Shopping in Costa Rica is not just about purchasing souvenirs; it's about immersing yourself in the culture and interacting with the craftsmen who pour their heart and soul into their work. Let me take you on a tour through some of the greatest areas to uncover these gems.

The Allure of Handmade Jewelry

My voyage started in the busy streets of San José, where I found myself fascinated by the beautiful patterns of handcrafted jewellery. Each item appeared to convey a tale, made with care and accuracy. One of my favourite sites was a modest store nestled away in a corner of the Central Market. The craftsman, a gentle old lady, described how she employed ancient methods handed down through generations to produce her magnificent works. I couldn't resist purchasing a set of earrings crafted from native stones, their brilliant hues reflecting the natural beauty of Costa Rica.

In the beach village of Tamarindo, I found a distinct sort of jewellery at the Tamarindo Night Market. Here, the designs were more contemporary, merging modern aesthetics with traditional materials. I met a young artist who utilised discarded materials to make her sculptures, each one unique and ecologically beneficial. Her enthusiasm for sustainability was motivating, and I left with a gorgeous bracelet that I still use to this day.

The Richness of Costa Rican Coffee

No vacation to Costa Rica would be complete without indulging in its world-renowned coffee. My voyage brought me to the beautiful coffee estates in the Central Valley, where I learnt about the complete process from bean to cup. Visiting a local coffee plantation was an eye-opening experience. The farmers were highly knowledgeable and enthusiastic about their art, and I acquired a fresh respect for the hard labour that goes into making each cup of coffee.

One of the pleasures was visiting a tiny family-run coffee business in Monteverde. The scent of freshly roasted beans filled the air as I went in, and I was welcomed with a warm grin by the proprietor. He took the time to explain the many sorts of coffee they provided and even gave me a demonstration of the ancient chorreador way of making coffee. I departed with a bag of their best beans, ready to duplicate the experience at home.

Unique Finds and Local Crafts

Exploring the marketplaces and stores of Costa Rica, I was always fascinated by the range of interesting treasures and local crafts. In the village of Sarchí, noted for its vivid painted oxcarts, I uncovered a treasure mine of wooden crafts. The craftspeople here are masters of their field, crafting anything from furniture to little trinkets with exquisite patterns. I couldn't resist purchasing a wonderfully carved wooden bowl, a fantastic centrepiece for my dining table.

In Manuel Antonio, I came into a wonderful business named Beso Loco business de Playa. The store was loaded with an unusual mix of beachwear, local crafts, and odd souvenirs. The proprietor, a lively and energetic lady, provided anecdotes about each item in her business. I ended up buying a hand-painted sarong and a vibrant beach bag, both of which have become mainstays in my summer outfit.

The Joy of Discovering Local Markets

One of the most exciting elements of shopping in Costa Rica is browsing the local markets. Each market has its own distinct character and gives a look into the everyday lives of the residents. The Central Market in San José is a lively centre of activity, with merchants selling everything from fresh fruit to handcrafted crafts. I liked meandering around the tiny aisles, absorbing in the sights and sounds, and speaking with the pleasant sellers.

In Tamarindo, the Tama Market was a highlight of my trip. Held every Saturday, this colourful market is a celebration of local culture and creativity. I spent hours perusing the vendors, enjoying excellent cuisine, and appreciating the handcrafted products. One of my favourite buys was a hand-painted porcelain cup, a lovely remembrance of my stay in Costa Rica.

Shopping in Costa Rica is an activity that goes beyond merely purchasing trinkets. It's about interacting with the local culture, supporting great artists, and finding unique items that you won't find anywhere else. Whether you're seeking handcrafted jewellery, rich coffee, or one-of-a-kind crafts, Costa Rica provides a shopping experience that is both enlightening and memorable.

Chapter Eleven: ITINERARIES AND TRAVEL TIPS

1 Day, 3 Day, 5 Day Suggested Itineraries

Planning a vacation to Costa Rica may be both thrilling and a little intimidating, considering the sheer amount of amazing sites to see and activities to enjoy. Whether you have only a day, a long weekend, or a full five days to visit, I've designed several itineraries based on my personal trips that will help you make the most of your time in this lovely nation.

1-Day Itinerary: A Taste of San José

If you just have one day in Costa Rica, spending time in the capital city of San José is a terrific opportunity to receive a fast but enriching flavour of the country's culture and history.

- **Morning**:

Start your day with a visit to the National Theatre, an architectural marvel in the centre of the city. The theatre's sumptuous décor and exquisite artwork give a look into Costa Rica's cultural past. Afterward, take a short walk to the Pre-Columbian Gold Museum, where you can marvel at the elaborate gold artefacts and learn about the indigenous civilizations of Costa Rica.

- **Afternoon**:

Head to the Central Market for lunch. This lively market is a sensory joy, featuring a range of traditional Costa Rican cuisine. I suggest tasting a casado, a classic dinner that includes rice, beans, plantains, salad, and your choice of meat. After lunch, go around the market to pick up some local crafts and souvenirs.

- **Evening**:

End your day with a visit to La Sabana Metropolitan Park, popularly referred to as the "lungs of San José." This vast green park is excellent for a leisurely stroll or just sitting and people-watching. If you have time, watch a show at the National

Theatre or have lunch at one of the city's many great eateries.

3-Day Itinerary: San José and Arenal

Within three days, you may see San José and journey out to one of Costa Rica's most renowned natural wonders, Arenal Volcano.

- **Day 1: San José**

Follow the one-day plan above to visit the attractions of San José.

- **Day 2: San José to Arenal**

In the morning, hire a vehicle or take a bus to La Fortuna, the entrance to Arenal Volcano. The journey takes roughly three hours and provides wonderful landscapes along the way. Once you arrive, check into your accommodation and travel directly to Arenal Volcano National Park. Spend the day exploring the paths and enjoying the spectacular views of the volcano. In the evening, unwind in one of the area's natural hot springs. I especially appreciated the hot springs in Tabacón, where the warm waters and green environs gave the ideal conclusion to an active day.

- **Day 3: Arenal**

Start your day with a visit to the Mistico Arenal Hanging Bridges Park. Walking over the suspension bridges high above the forest floor was an amazing experience, affording new viewpoints of the rainforest and its fauna. Afterward, travel to La Fortuna Waterfall for a refreshing dip. The climb down to the waterfall is tough but well worth the effort. In the afternoon, you may pick between a zip-lining excursion or a visit to the Arenal Observatory Lodge for further hiking and birding. Return to San José in the evening or spend another night in La Fortuna if your itinerary permits.

5-Day Itinerary: San José, Arenal, and Monteverde

Within five days, you may tour San José, Arenal, and the cloud forests of Monteverde, providing you a well-rounded understanding of Costa Rica's different landscapes.

- **Day 1: San José**

Follow the one-day schedule to discover San José.

- **Day 2: San José to Arenal**

Drive or take a shuttle to La Fortuna and spend the day touring Arenal Volcano National Park and resting in the hot springs.

- **Day 3: Arenal**

Spend the day at Mistico Arenal Hanging Bridges Park and La Fortuna Waterfall, with optional zip-lining or birding in the afternoon.

- **Day 4: Arenal to Monteverde**

In the morning, go to Monteverde, a route that takes around three hours by vehicle or bus. The route includes a magnificent boat ride over Lake Arenal, which was one of the highlights of my vacation. Once you arrive in Monteverde, check into your accommodation and tour the Monteverde Cloud Forest Reserve. The reserve's well-maintained pathways and rich flora and animals make it a must-visit. In the evening, try taking a guided night walk to witness the forest's nocturnal inhabitants.

- **Day 5: Monteverde**

Start your day with a visit to the Monteverde Butterfly Garden, where you can learn about the numerous varieties of butterflies and other insects endemic to the region. Next, walk to the Monteverde Orchid Garden to observe a magnificent array of orchids. In the afternoon, visit the Selvatura Adventure Park for a canopy tour or a stroll along the hanging bridges. If you have time, stop by the Monteverde Cheese Factory for a tour and some tasty samples before travelling back to San José.

These itineraries provide a combination of cultural experiences, natural beauty, and adventure, ensuring that you make the most of your time in Costa Rica, whether you have one day or five. Each day is filled with activities that highlight the best of what this beautiful nation has to offer.

Essentials for Every Season (Packing and Activities)

When I initially began planning my vacation to Costa Rica, I immediately realised that packing for this varied nation needed a little forethought. With its varying temperatures and many activities, knowing what to carry and what to do in each season may make all the difference. Here's a tip based on my personal experiences, to help you pack intelligently and enjoy every second of your Costa Rican journey.

Dry Season (December to April)

Packing Essentials:
The dry season, also known as the high season, is characterised by bright days and low rainfall. This is a great time to visit the beaches and national parks.

- **Lightweight Clothing**: Pack breathable, lightweight garments like shorts, t-shirts, and sundresses. The temperatures may reach fairly high, particularly in coastal places.

- **Swimsuit:** With so many lovely beaches and hot springs, you'll want to have your swimsuit available.
- **Sun Protection:** Sunscreen, sunglasses, and a wide-brimmed hat are needed to protect oneself from the powerful tropical sun.
- **-Comfortable Footwear:** Bring sandals for the beach and sturdy hiking shoes for touring national parks and volcanoes.
- **Reusable Water Bottle:** Staying hydrated is crucial, particularly during outdoor activity.

Activities:

- **Beach Hopping:** The dry season is great for exploring Costa Rica's gorgeous beaches. I spent days relaxing on the dunes of Manuel Antonio and Tamarindo, swimming in the pristine seas, and trying my hand at surfing.
- **Hiking:** With beautiful sky and dry paths, it's the ideal time for trekking. I adored touring Arenal Volcano National Park and the Monteverde Cloud Forest Reserve.
- **Wildlife Watching:** This season is fantastic for observing wildlife, since animals are more active and easier to view. I had

several remarkable experiences with monkeys, sloths, and beautiful birds.

Green Season (May to November)

Packing Essentials:

The green season, or rainy season, delivers beautiful vistas and fewer visitors. While it does rain regularly, the showers are typically brief and followed by sunlight.

- **Rain Gear:** A lightweight, waterproof jacket and a travel umbrella are must-haves. I also brought a rain cover for my bag.
- **Quick-Dry Clothing:** Opt for quick-dry materials that can endure the humidity and occasional downpours.
- **Insect Repellent:** The rain brings out the insects, so insect repellent is vital.
- **Waterproof Footwear:** Waterproof hiking boots or shoes are perfect for muddy paths and damp circumstances.
- **Layers:** The weather may be unpredictable, so carrying layers helps you adapt to shifting temperatures.

Activities:

- **Waterfalls and Hot Springs:** The rains make the waterfalls even more magnificent. I visited La Fortuna Waterfall and loved the refreshing hot springs nearby.
- **Surfing:** The green season delivers stronger waves, making it an excellent period for surfing. I had a blast catching waves in Jaco and Dominical.
- **Eco-Tours:** This is the perfect season to explore the rainforests and enjoy eco-tours. The lush foliage and lively fauna are at their height. I attended a guided trip in Corcovado National Park and was surprised by the wildlife.

Year-Round Essentials

Regardless of the season, there are a few things that I found important during my trip:

- **Travel Insurance:** Always a good idea to get travel insurance that covers medical emergencies and trip cancellations.
- **First Aid Kit:** A simple first aid kit containing band-aids, antiseptic wipes, and any personal prescriptions.

- - Portable Charger: Keeping your gadgets charged is vital, particularly when you're out exploring all day.
- **Camera:** Costa Rica is highly picturesque, so having a decent camera or smartphone to record the moments is essential.
- **Local Currency:** While credit cards are commonly accepted, carrying some Costa Rican colones for little transactions and gratuities is useful.

Seasonal Activities

Dry Season Highlights:

- - **Festivals:** The dry season is crowded with festivals and activities. I visited the Palmares Festival in January, which was a spectacular celebration with music, dancing, and traditional cuisine.
- - **Snorkeling and Diving:** The pristine waters during the dry season are great for snorkelling and diving. I visited the underwater environment at Caño Island and was amazed by the aquatic life.

Green Season Highlights:

Turtle Nesting: The green season is the time to watch sea turtles breeding on the beaches. I visited Tortuguero National Park and watched in astonishment as the turtles came ashore to deposit their eggs.

- **River Rafting:** The flooded rivers during the wet season provide for spectacular white-water rafting. I had an adrenaline-pumping excursion on the Pacuare River.

Packing for Costa Rica involves a little forethought, but with the correct gear and a spirit of adventure, you'll be ready to experience all this beautiful nation has to offer, no matter the season. Each season delivers its own unique experiences, making Costa Rica a year-round destination that never fails to surprise.

Chapter Twelve: FINAL THOUGHTS

What Makes Costa Rica Special

As my adventure through Costa Rica drew to a conclusion, I found myself wondering what made this nation so remarkable. It wasn't only the magnificent vistas or the wonderful fauna, but something deeper that made a lasting effect on me. Here are my concluding views on what makes Costa Rica so remarkable.

The Spirit of "Pura Vida"

One of the first things I noticed upon landing in Costa Rica was the omnipresent term "Pura Vida." It's more than simply a statement; it's a way of life. Translated as "pure life," it symbolises the Costa Rican attitude to living with pleasure, simplicity, and thankfulness. Whether I was welcomed by a native or just witnessing regular interactions, the spirit of Pura Vida was there. It reminded me to calm down, cherish the moment, and accept the beauty of life.

The Warmth of the People

The kindness and generosity of the Costa Rican people, or Ticos, is something I will never forget. From the minute I arrived, I was greeted with open arms. Whether I was asking for directions, shopping at a local market, or enjoying a meal, the generosity and hospitality of the residents made me feel at home. I recall a specific event in a little town near Monteverde, when a family asked me to join them for supper. We exchanged tales, laughs, and excellent homemade food. It was times like this that made my vacation very unique.

The Diverse Landscapes

Costa Rica's various landscapes are nothing short of magnificent. From the gorgeous beaches of the Pacific and Caribbean coastlines to the lush jungles and towering volcanoes, the nation provides a spectacular diversity of natural splendour. Each area has its own distinct charm and character. I was intrigued by the misty cloud forests of Monteverde, the stunning lava plains of Arenal, and the tranquil beaches of Manuel Antonio. The sheer diversity of scenery made every day an adventure, with new delights to uncover around every turn.

The Abundance of Wildlife

Costa Rica is a delight for nature aficionados. The country's dedication to conservation and sustainable tourism has created a shelter for a varied variety of animals. I was lucky enough to observe monkeys swinging through the trees, sloths relaxing in the canopy, and colourful birds fluttering around. One of the highlights of my vacation was a guided night tour in Corcovado National Park, where I glimpsed a tapir and heard the distant scream of howler monkeys. The chance to watch these creatures in their native environment was a humbling and awe-inspiring experience.

The Commitment to Sustainability

Costa Rica's devotion to sustainability and environmental protection is very impressive. The government has made considerable advances in conserving its natural resources and developing eco-friendly activities. I was amazed by the various eco-lodges, organic farms, and conservation programs I visited. Visiting a coffee plantation that utilised sustainable agricultural practices and staying at eco-friendly hotels made me more mindful of my personal influence on the environment. Costa Rica's attempts to conserve its natural beauty for future generations are a tribute to its forward-thinking and ethical approach to tourism.

The Rich Cultural Heritage

Costa Rica's rich cultural legacy is woven into the fabric of daily life. From traditional music and dance to colourful festivals and delectable food, the country's culture is a celebration of its history and variety. I had the pleasure of visiting a local festival in a tiny town, where I witnessed traditional dances, listened to live music, and enjoyed local specialties. The pleasure and enthusiasm with which the Ticos shared their culture was contagious, and I felt blessed to be a part of it, even if only for a short time.

The Sense of Adventure

Costa Rica is a paradise for adventure lovers. Whether it's zip-lining through the trees, white-water rafting down a rushing river, or trekking up a volcano, the nation provides unlimited options for thrill and adventure. I enjoyed the spirit of adventure, undertaking things

I had never done before and pushing my limitations. The adrenaline rush of zip-lining in Monteverde and the pleasure of surfing in Tamarindo are experiences that will remain with me forever.

As I boarded my trip home, I realised that Costa Rica had offered me more than simply lovely images and trinkets. It has given me a revitalised respect for nature, a stronger awareness of sustainability, and a heart full of amazing memories. Costa Rica is remarkable not merely because of its natural beauties, but because of the spirit of its people and the ideals they hold dear. It's a location that urges you to live completely, enjoy the present, and bring a bit of Pura Vida with you wherever you go.

Leaving Costa Rica: Souvenirs and Memories

As I relax on the balcony of my comfortable little cottage, the sun starts its set, spreading a golden colour over the beautiful Costa Rican countryside. The subtle rustling of palm leaves and the distant cry of exotic birds create a harmony that I know I shall miss greatly. My stay in Costa Rica has been nothing short of spectacular, and as I prepare to leave, I find myself reminiscing on the keepsakes and memories that will long remind me of this beautiful nation.

One of the first things I did was visit the lively marketplaces of San José. The Mercado Central, with its maze of vendors, was a treasure trove of local goods and foods. I couldn't resist buying up a gorgeously hand-painted oxcart miniature, a symbol of Costa Rica's rich agricultural tradition. Each brushstroke conveyed a narrative, and I knew it would be a fantastic centrepiece for my living room back home.

In the beach village of Tamarindo, I came across a modest boutique maintained by a local craftsman. Here, I discovered magnificent jewellery crafted from volcanic rock and polished seashells. The works were not only gorgeous but also embodied the sense of Costa Rica's natural beauty. I picked a beautiful necklace that seemed to catch the very essence of the ocean, a memento of the numerous hours I spent basking in the sun and surfing the waves.

Of course, no vacation to Costa Rica would be complete without drinking its world-renowned coffee. I visited a coffee farm in the Central Valley, where I learnt about the laborious process of producing, harvesting, and roasting coffee beans. The wonderful scent of freshly brewed coffee filled the air, and I couldn't resist purchasing several bags to take home. Each taste would bring me back to the beautiful hills and the warmth of the Tico welcome.

As I pack my bag, I carefully wrap a vivid handmade blanket I bought in the mountains of Monteverde. The elaborate designs and vibrant colours are a monument to the talent and ingenuity of the indigenous weavers. This blanket will not only keep me warm on cold evenings but also act as a concrete link to the cloud forests and the tremendous biodiversity I experienced there.

Beyond the tangible gifts, the memories I've formed in Costa Rica are the most priceless of all. I remember the exhilaration of zip-lining through the canopy, the awe-inspiring vista of Arenal Volcano, and the tranquil moments spent in natural hot springs. The laughs shared with newfound friends, the taste of fresh ceviche at the beach, and the beautiful sunsets over the Pacific Ocean remain imprinted in my memories forever.

Leaving Costa Rica is bittersweet. While I'm delighted to come home and share my travels with loved ones, a part of me will always crave for the pura vida lifestyle. This voyage has been transforming, and the mementos I've acquired are more than simply items; they are recollections of the experiences, the people, and the beauty that characterise Costa Rica.

As I lock my luggage and take one final glance at the stunning scenery, I know that Costa Rica has left an everlasting impact on my heart. The keepsakes and memories will act as a bridge, linking me to this beautiful area until I can come once again.

Conclusion regarding Costa Rica's Natural and Cultural Wonders

As I sit on the brink of a quiet riverbank, the soothing murmur of the water harmonises with the distant sounds of howler monkeys, producing a symphony that encompasses the spirit of Costa Rica. My voyage across this fascinating place has been a tapestry of bright experiences, each thread woven with the natural and cultural beauties that make this country so special.

Costa Rica's natural splendour is nothing short of spectacular. One of my most unforgettable excursions was trekking through the deep, mist-laden Monteverde Cloud Forest. The air was dense with the aroma of dirt and greenery, and every step revealed a new wonder. From the delicate orchids hanging to old trees to the elusive dazzling quetzal flying over the canopy, the forest seemed like a live, breathing organism. It was here that I finally realised the concept of biodiversity, as the forest teemed with life in every corner.

The volcanic vistas of Costa Rica are equally awe-inspiring. Standing at the foot of Arenal Volcano, I felt a feeling of wonder and admiration for the sheer force of nature. The volcano, with its precise conical form, rose magnificently against the sky, a reminder of the dynamic forces that create our globe. The surrounding region, with its hot springs and rich foliage, created a dramatic contrast to the rough volcanic topography, creating a unique and intriguing atmosphere.

Costa Rica's beaches are another attraction of this diversified nation. The beautiful beaches of Manuel Antonio National Park provided a fantastic background for leisure and discovery. I spent hours snorkelling in the crystal-clear waters, marvelling at the beautiful coral reefs and the multitude of aquatic creatures that called them home. The sunsets here were nothing short of magnificent, painting the sky in shades of orange, pink, and purple, and leaving me in a sense of quiet pleasure.

Beyond its natural beauty, Costa Rica's cultural legacy is rich and firmly anchored in tradition. I had the honour of visiting a little town where I was greeted with open arms by the local inhabitants. They shared their rituals, tales, and excellent food with me, providing an insight into their way of life. The friendliness and generosity of the Tico people made a lasting impact on me, and I felt a genuine connection to their culture.

One of the most exciting cultural experiences was attending a traditional dance performance. The dancers, draped in vivid costumes, danced smoothly to the beat of marimba music. Each dance presented a tale, representing the history and spirit of the Costa Rican people. It was a celebration of life, love, and tenacity, and I felt proud to be a part of it.

As I prepare to leave Costa Rica, I am flooded with a feeling of appreciation for the experiences and memories I have accumulated. This voyage has been a remarkable reminder of the beauty and variety of our globe. Costa Rica's natural and cultural beauties have left an everlasting impact on my heart, and I know that the lessons and experiences from this journey will remain with me forever.

Costa Rica is a place of exceptional beauty and rich cultural legacy. From its lush rainforests and magnificent volcanoes to its clean beaches and thriving customs, every part of this nation is a monument to the beauty of nature and the tenacity of its people. As I wave goodbye to this beautiful location, I bring with me not only trinkets, but a profound appreciation for the beauty that is Costa Rica.

Printed in Great Britain
by Amazon